Bhagavad Gītā for the 21st Century

Before introducing this simplified 21st century translation of the sublime teachings of Lord Krishna's *Bhagavad Gītā* to Hindus and followers of other faith, I scrutinizingly studied the translations and commentaries of some prominent scholars. The author, I am indebted to, are Swami Chidbhavananda and Bhaktivedanta Swami Prabhupada.

These divine teachings constitute a matchless heritage that has been passed down since time immemorial from Lord Krishna to Vivasvan (the Sun-god) to Manu (the father of mankind) to us today. A heritage that was confined to the whole world and should be taken advantage of and not to be missed in one's lifetime.

> "I shall teach you such knowledge endowed with the right understanding knowing which nothing else shall remain to be known in this world. Ch. 7, v. 2.
>
> There is nothing higher than Me, O conqueror of wealth. Everything is strung on Me like pearls on a thread. Ch. 7, v. 7.
>
> I am the Lord, your goal, maintainer, witness, abode, refuge, and good-hearted friend. I am the cause of existence, the dissolution, province of the demi-gods, place of rest and the imperishable seed. Ch. 9, v. 18.
>
> I am the origin of all. From Me everything arises. The wise know this and adore Me with great attention." Ch. 10, v. 8.

My translation is based on the Bhishmaparvan, the sixth book of *Mahabharata*. I looked into every word, ensuring it conveyed the exact meaning into English.

Navin Nunkoo was born in Mauritius. He took World Affairs, Religious Studies and Journalism for his education in English.

In 1974 he wrote the book *A Gleam of Light* which was published in London. Thereafter Navin went on to dedicate his time to study the Vedic classics of ancient India especially Lord Krishna's *Bhagavad Gītā* (Song of God).

BHAGAVAD GĪTĀ

for the 21st Century

Navin Nunkoo

DEV BOOKS

ISBN 81-89835-00-9
First published 2006

Typeset, printed and published by
DEV BOOKS,
11-B Court Road,
Delhi-110 054,
email: devbooks@vsnl.net

Contents

Preface

Thousands of years before conquering nations would rise and fall, the ancient land of India was graced by the first dawn of civilisation on planet earth. *Dharma,* following the laws of God, was at its height.

Saints, sages, monarchs, administrators, warriors, philosophers and the general populace all left the hallmarks of divine deeds. But as time passed the forces of evil, in the form of envious and hateful people threatened to destabilize *dharma.* Irreligion came into being, degrading acts were performed and suffering increased.

Thus in His eighth incarnation the Supreme Godhead, Lord Vishnu, Krishna, descended in this material world to restore *dharma.* Here at Kuruksetra between the two armies, the righteous Pandavas and the unrighteous Kauravas, poised for the epic battle, Lord Krishna, creator and sustainer of all the three worlds, mercifully imparts wisdom in all its magnanimity again to the human race, now through His disciple Prince Arjuna, son of Pandu, showing the path of *dharma.*

This spoken science of Lord Krishna, heritage of the world, compiled into seven hundred verses in the Bhagavad Gita by the celestial sage Vyasa, unveils the splendour of unparalleled mystery. Immortality is attainable. The prescribed theories in the sacred texts, if practised, remain the sure means indeed.

"Nothing is sustainable without Me in all the worlds. I am the air that you breathe. I am gravity. I am life and I am death. No one surpasses Me. I am the primeval seed. I was never born. I have created the four divisions in society. I dwell in everybody's heart. I am a friend to all beings. I do not discriminate." So says Lord Krishna.

All those who persevere positively in the study and practice of the wisdom of Bhagavad Gita will surely find light.

As for me, after training at the London School of Journalism, being instrumental in bringing forth this twenty-first century translation of Bhagavad Gita has given me joy beyond the measure of all earthly riches.

Introduction

Lord Krishna:

Creator of wisdom and ignorance

Of light and darkness

Of time and space

Master builder and destroyer

Forgiver and punisher

Abode of heaven and hell

Commander of all the elements

Seed of all that lives

And in Whom lies all salvation.

Acknowledgements

It gives me great pleasure to express my debt of gratitude to Caroline Vieira Bhogini for her invaluable suggestions in editing my translation, my son Nitesh from whom the idea for the new version originated, my daughter Nishpa Venusah for the textual criticism and my wife Indira for her active help in typing the manuscript.

I was born and educated in Mauritius. Since my arrival in United Kingdom, I made the most of the British education and made myself more aware of Lord Krishna's spiritual teachings.

Although it remains beyond all the three worlds to know the Supreme Lord completely, it is exciting to realise that knowing Him even partly, and complying with Him, will lead humanity to freedom from the cycle of rebirths. With a deep sense of responsibility, I have made every effort to bring clarity to the verses for the elucidation of the readers. Mistakes, misrepresentations or omissions, if any, are mine alone.

Acknowledgements

Summary

Chapter One
Arjuna Overwhelmed with Compassion

As the Kuru and Pandava armies prepare for battle Sanjaya, who is gifted with mystic vision, describes to the blind king Dhrtarastra the events taking place at Kuruksetra. Lord Krishna drives Arjuna's chariot between the two armies where Arjuna sees family members, relatives and teachers. Arjuna's heart falters out of compassion.

Chapter Two
A Summary of the Bhagavad Gītā

Arjuna, as disciple, questions Lord Krishna before the battle. What follows is the highest conversation between God and man as the Supreme imparts wisdom again to the universe, paving the way with wisdom for all people to attain eternal life.

Chapter Three
The *Yoga* of Action

The Lord describes two paths, that of philosophical knowledge and that of action. Since all people are obliged to act according to their natural qualities, Krishna recommends action to be performed for the pleasure of the Lord, without attachment. The real enemies of mankind are desire and anger.

Chapter Four
The Highest Mystery

Krishna describes the history of Bhagavad Gita and how He descends Himself periodically to re-establish its message. There are four divisions of human qualities with activities prescribed for each, which free one from the laws of karma.

Chapter Five
Renunciation of the Fruits of Action

By performing religious acts the ascetic achieves spiritual understanding in this world, and peace and absorption in God.

Chapter Six
Deep, Abstract *Yoga* Meditation

Asceticism, the practice of yoga for self-purification, leads to freedom from desire, immunity from sorrow, bliss and union with God. One who falls from yoga practice takes birth again to continue in the next life. Of all *yogis* the most dear is the devotee.

Chapter Seven
The *Yoga* of Sacred Knowledge

Knowledge of how the Lord is present in every element of nature, the universe, the sacred mantras, our qualities and attitudes is described. There are four kinds of people recognised by Krishna who find liberation in this way, whereas the ignorant become more entangled in material nature.

Chapter Eight
Attaining the Imperishable

By being fully absorbed in meditating on the Supreme spirit in life one transcends the constantly remanifesting world and attains the perfected state at death, beyond the cycle of rebirth.

Chapter Nine
The Highest Mystical Knowledge

Krishna is the imperishable originator of all beings. He is everything, the beneficiary of all sacrifices and the goal of all worship. By worshipping Him with love one will attain Him.

Chapter Ten
The Omnipresent Lord

Krishna details how He can be recognised in every aspect of the universal manifestation, which He supports with just a fractional part of Himself. His glories are endless. He illuminates the minds of those who recognise this and are constantly devoted to Him.

Chapter Eleven
The Universal Form

To fulfil Arjuna's desire Krishna gives him divine eyes to see His universal form. Arjuna then sees a fearsome form without beginning or end, within which are all things, all the demigods, all the fleeing demons and all the soldiers dieing in battle. The form is ferocious and terrifying and Arjuna pays his homage and requests to see again the Lord's gentle, two-armed form.

Chapter Twelve
Union Through Devotion

The Lord describes two paths to union with God, the impersonal and the devotional, but recommends the path of devotion. There are several alternatives for those who are unable, but He declares that the devotee is most dear to Him.

Chapter Thirteen
The Field, the Knower of the Field and Nature

Lord Krishna explains that the body is the field, the knower is the individual soul and Krishna dwelling within the heart, pervading all, is the knower in all fields. One can approach the Supreme knowing what is knowledge; how the soul and the Supreme soul can be perceived; what is nature, its qualities and transformation; and about cause and effect.

Chapter Fourteen
The Three Qualities of Material Nature

Wisdom is first to understand the interactions of the three modes of material nature and how to overcome their influence. One can then become established in eternal truth and bliss.

Chapter Fifteen
The Secrets of the Supreme

The universe is described as a great tree of entanglement which needs to be cut down with the axe of detachment. The living entities struggle with the material senses but the Supreme is present in everything, and perceiving this one's endeavours can become perfect.

Chapter Sixteen
Two Kinds of Human Nature

The Lord describes the qualities of one born with divine nature and also those with the demoniac nature. Following the path of sense gratification, under the spell of delusion, they fall into the demoniac races, through the gates of hell, desire, anger and greed, into the lowest mode of existence. Therefore, one should let scripture be the guide for correct action.

Chapter Seventeen
Three Kinds of Faith

There are three kinds of faith, foodstuffs, sacrifices, austerities, charity and sacred syllables for the performance of religious activities.

Chapter Eighteen
Renunciation and Detachment

Krishna concludes by describing the three kinds of actions, the five causes of action, the three kinds of knowledge, qualities, intelligence, determination, happiness and duties. By following the activities of one's nature one can achieve success, perfection, and through devotion one can attain the eternal, blissful abode of the Lord. So ends this greatest conversation of all time between the Supreme Lord and man.

Chapter One

Arjuna Overwhelmed with Compassion

As the Kuru and Pandava armies prepare for battle Sanjaya, who is gifted with mystic vision, describes to the blind king Dhritarashtra the events taking place at Kurukshetra. Lord Krishna drives Arjuna's chariot between the two armies where Arjuna sees family members, relatives and teachers. Arjuna's heart falters out of compassion.

Dhṛtarāṣṭra uvāca

1. *dharma-kṣetre kuru-kṣetre*
samavetā yuyutsavaḥ
māmakāḥ pāṇḍavāś caiva
kim akurvata sañjaya

Sañjaya uvāca

2. *dṛṣṭvā tu pāṇḍavānīkaṁ*
vyūḍhaṁ duryodhanas tadā
ācāryam upasaṁgamya
rājā vacanam abravīt

3. *paśyaitāṁ pāṇḍu-putrāṇām*
ācārya mahatīṁ camūm
vyūḍhāṁ drupada-putreṇa
tava śiṣyeṇa dhīmatā

4. *atra śūrā maheṣv-āsā*
bhīmārjuna-samā yudhi
yuyudhāno virātaś ca
drupadaś ca mahā-rathaḥ

5. *dhṛṣṭaketuś cekitānaḥ*
kāśirājaś ca vīryavān
purujit kuntibhojaś ca
śaibyaś ca nara-pungavaḥ

6. *yudhāmanyuś ca vikrānta*
uttamaujāś ca vīryavān
saubhadro draupadeyāś ca
sarva eva mahā-rathāḥ

7. *asmākaṁ tu viśiṣṭā ye*
tān nibodha dvijottama
nāyakā mama sainyasya
saṁjñārthaṁ tān bravīmi te

Dhritarashtra said:

1. At Kurukshetra, in the field of action, my army and the army of Pandu met, ready to do the battle. What did they do Sanjaya?

Sanjaya said:

2. Prince Duryodhana surveyed the Pandava army arranged for battle, then went to his teacher Drona and spoke these words.

3. Master, look at the mighty army of Pandu's sons arranged by your learned disciple, the son of Drupada.

4. There are learned men and mighty bowmen, equal in battle to Arjuna and Bhima, such as Yuyudhana, Virata and Drupada, the great chariot fighter.

5. Dhrstaketu, Cekitana and the valiant king of Kasi, Purujit, Kuntibhoja and Saibya, the excellent hero.

6. The courageous Yudhamanyu, the powerful Uttamauja, the son of Subhadra, the sons of Draupadi—all are great chariot-fighters.

7. But know, O best of the Brahmanas, of all those distinguished chiefs who are the commanders of my army. Let me name them for your information.

8. *bhavān bhīṣmaś ca karṇaś ca*
kṛpaś ca samitiṁ-jayaḥ
aśvatthāmā vikarṇaś ca
saumadattis tathaiva ca

9. *anye ca bahavaḥ śūrā*
mad-arthe tyakta-jīvitāḥ
nānā-śastra-praharaṇāḥ
sarve yuddha-viśāradāḥ

10. *aparyāptaṁ tad asmākaṁ*
balaṁ bhīṣmābhirakṣitam
paryāptaṁ tv idam eteṣāṁ
balaṁ bhīsmābhirakṣitam

11. *ayaneṣu ca sarveṣu*
yathā-bhāgam avasthitāḥ
bhīṣmam evābhirakṣantu
bhavantaḥ sarva eva hi

12. *tasya sañjanayan harṣaṁ*
kuru-vṛddhaḥ pitāmahaḥ
siṁha-nādaṁ vinadyoccaiḥ
śaṅkhaṁ dadhumau pratāpavān

13. *tataḥ śaṅkhās ca bheryaś ca*
paṇavānaka-gomukhāḥ
sahasaivābhyahanyanta
sa śabdas tumulo' bhavat

14. *tatah śvetair hayair yukte*
mahati syandane sthitau
mādhavaḥ pāṇḍavaś caiva
divyau śaṅkhau pradadhmatuḥ

15. *pāñcajanyaṁ hṛṣīkeśo*
devadattaṁ dhanañjayaḥ
pauṇḍraṁ dadhmau mahā-śaṅkhaṁ
bhima-karmā vṛkodaraḥ

8. Yourself, Bhishma, Karna, the victorious Kripa, Asvatthama, Vikarna and the son of Somadatta.

9. And there are many other heroes who are ready to die for me. Armed with various weapons, they are all skilful in war.

10. Our army is huge and commanded by Bhishma. But their army, commanded by Bhima, is small.

11. And now, let all of you, from your respective places, in whatever division you are stationed, protect Bhishma.

12. Then the valiant Bhishma, the Kuru elder, blew his conch-shell loudly. It roared like a lion delighting Duryodhana.

13. Then suddenly, conch-shells, drums, tabors, horns were sounded forth and the noise grew tumultuous.

14. Seated in their great war-chariot yoked to white horses, Lord Krishna and Arjuna, the son of Pandu, blew their divine conch-shells.

15. Lord Krishna blew His conch-shell, the Panchajanya. Arjuna blew the Devadatta, "God given," and the dreadful, wolf-bellied Bhima blew his great conch-shell, Paundram.

16. *anantavijayaṁ rājā*
kuntī-putro yudhiṣṭhiraḥ
nakulaḥ sahadevaś ca
sughoṣa-maṇipuṣpakau

17. *kāśyaś ca parameṣv-āsaḥ*
śikhaṇḍī ca mahā-rathaḥ
dhṛṣṭadyumno virāṭaś ca
sātyakiś cāparājitaḥ

18. *drupado draupadeyāś ca*
sarvaśaḥ pṛthivī-pate
saubhadraś ca mahā-bāhuḥ
śaṅkhān dadhmuḥ pṛthak pṛthak

19. *sa ghoṣo dhārtarāṣṭrāṇāṁ*
hṛdayāni vyadārayat
nabhaś ca pṛthivīṁ caiva
tumulo vyanunādayan

20 *atha vyavasthitān dṛṣṭvā*
dhārtarāṣṭrān kapi-dhvajaḥ
pravṛtte śastra-sampāte
dhanur udyamya pāṇḍavaḥ
hṛṣīkeśaṁ tadā vākyam
idam āha mahī-pate

Arjuna uvāca

21. *senayor ubhayor madhye*
rathaṁ sthāpaya me' cyuta

22. *yāvad etān nirikṣe' haṁ*
yoddhu-kāmān avasthitān
kair mayā saha yoddhavyam
asmin raṇa-samudyame

23. *yotsyamānān avekṣe' haṁ*
ya ete' tra samāgatāḥ
dhārtarāṣṭrasya durbuddher
yuddhe priya-cikīrṣavaḥ

16. King Yudhishthira, Kunti's son, blew Anantavijaya, "Eternal Victory," Nakula blew Sughosha, "Pleasant Sound" and Sahadeva blew the Manipushpaka, "Gem Flower."

17. The king of Kasi, the excellent archer, Sikhandi, the great warrior, Dhrishtadyumna, Virata and the invincible Satyaki.

18. Drupada, king of the Panchalas, Draupadi's sons and Abhimanyu—the mighty armed son of Subhadra, all blew their conch-shells one by one, O king.

19. That tumultuous uproar shook the hearts of Dhritarashtra's sons and reverberated through heaven and earth.

20. Arjuna, bearing the sign of Hanuman on his banner, looked upon Dhritarashtra's sons drawn up in battle. Fighting was about to begin. He lifted his bow, then O king, spoke these words to Krishna.

Arjuna said:

21-22. O Imperishable One, draw my chariot between the two armies so that I may see those warriors standing there, with whom I must fight in this war.

23. Let me look at those who have come here to fight, eager to please the weak-minded son of Dhritarashtra in battle.

Sañjaya uvāca

24. *evam ukto hṛṣīkeśo*
guḍākeśena bhārata
senayor ubhayor madhye
sthāpayitvā rathottamam

25. *bhīṣma-droṇa-pramukhataḥ*
sarveṣāṁ ca mahī-kṣitām
uvāca pārtha paśyaitān
samavetān kurūn iti

26. *tatrāpaśyat sthitān pārthaḥ*
pitṝn atha pitāmahān
ācāryān mātulān bhrātṝn
putrān pautrān sakhīṁs tathā
śvaśurān suhṛdaś caiva
senayor ubhayor api

27. *tān samīkṣya sa kaunteyaḥ*
sarvān bandhūn avasthitān
kṛpayā parayāviṣṭo
viṣīdann idam abravīt

Arjuna uvāca

28. *dṛṣṭvemaṁ sva-janaṁ kṛṣṇa*
yuyutsuṁ samupasthitam
sīdanti mama gātrāṇi
mukham ca pariśuṣyati

29. *vepathuś ca śarīre me*
roma-harṣaś ca jāyate
gāṇḍīvaṁ sraṁsate hastāt
tvak caiva paridahyate

30. *na ca śaknamy avasthātum*
bhramatīva ca me manaḥ
nimittāni ca paśyāmi
viparītāni keśava

Sanjaya said:

24. O descendent of Bharata, at Arjuna's request Lord Krishna brought the fine chariot between the two armies.

25. In front of Bhishma, Drona and all the rulers of earth, He said, "See Partha, all the Kurus are assembled here."

26. There Arjuna saw standing in both armies fathers, grandfathers, teachers, uncles, brothers, grandsons, good-hearted friends and fathers-in-law.

27. Seeing all these kinsmen standing near, the son of Kunti, filled with deep sentiment, sadly spoke.

Arjuna said:

28. O Krishna, seeing all these kinsmen arrayed, eager for battle, my limbs fail me and my mouth goes dry.

29. My body trembles
My hair stands on end
My bow slips from my hand
And my skin burns.

30. I am unable to stand; my mind is reeling and I see bleak omens, O Keshava.

31. *na ca śreyo' nupaśyāmi*
hatvā sva-janam āhave
na kāṅkṣe vijayaṁ kṛṣṇa
na ca rājyaṁ sukhāni ca

32. *kiṁ no rājyena govinda*
kiṁ bhogair jīvitena vā

33. *yeṣām arthe kāṅkṣitaṁ no*
rājyaṁ bhogāḥ sukhāni ca
ta ime' vasthitā yuddhe
prāṇāṁs tyaktvā dhanāni ca

34. *ācāryāḥ pitaraḥ putrās*
tathaiva ca pitāmahāḥ
mātulāḥ śvaśurāḥ pautrāḥ
śyālāḥ sambandhinas tathā

35. *etān na hantum icchāmi*
ghnato' pi madhusūdana
api trailokya-rājyasya
hetoḥ kiṁ nu mahī-kṛte

36. *nihatya dhārtarāṣṭrān naḥ*
kā prītiḥ syāj janārdana
pāpam evāśrayed asmān
hatvaitān ātatāyinaḥ

37. *tasmān nārhā vayaṁ hantuṁ*
dhārtarāṣṭrān sva-bāndhavān
sva-janaṁ hi kathaṁ hatvā
sukhinaḥ syāma mādhava

38. *yady apy ete na paśyanti*
lobhopahata-cetasaḥ
kula-kṣaya-kṛtaṁ doṣaṁ
mitra-drohe ca pātakam

31. I can see nothing good arising from slaying my kinsmen in this conflict O Krishna, neither do I desire victory, sovereignty nor prosperity.

32. What use is a kingdom to us, or prosperity, or life, Govinda?

33. Here standing in battle are those for whose sake we would desire kingdoms, prosperity and happiness, prepared to give up their lives and wealth.

34. There are my teachers, fathers, sons, grandfathers, uncles, fathers-in-law, grandsons, brothers-in-law and other kinsmen.

35. Were I to be killed by them, O Madhusudana, I still would not wish to kill them, not even for sovereignty over the three worlds, and certainly not for the earth.

36. What joy can we get, O Janardana, if we destroy Dhritarashtra's sons? We will only incur sin if we kill these aggressors.

37. It is, therefore, not right to slay Dhritarashtra's sons, and our friends, for how could we, O Madhava, be happy after slaying our own kinsmen?

38. Their intellect is misled by greed and they cannot see the evil in the destruction of a family nor the sin of hostility against friends.

39. *kathaṁ na jñeyam asmābhiḥ*
pāpād asmān nivartitum
kula-kṣaya-kṛtaṁ doṣaṁ
prapaśyadbhir janārdana

40. *kula-kṣaye praṇaśyanti*
kula-dharmāḥ sanātanāḥ
dharme naṣṭe kulam kṛtsnam
adharmo' bhibhavaty uta

41. *adharmābhibhavāt kṛṣṇa*
praduṣyanti kula-striyaḥ
strīṣu duṣṭāsu varṣṇeya
jāyate varṇa-sankaraḥ

42. *saṅkaro narakāyaiva*
kula-ghnānāṁ kulasya ca
patanti pitaro hy eṣāṁ
lupta-piṇḍodaka-kriyāḥ

43. *doṣair etaiḥ kula-ghnānāṁ*
varṇa-saṅkara-kārakaiḥ
utsādyante jāti-dharmāḥ
kalu-dharmāś ca śāśvatāḥ

44. *utsanna-kula-dharmāṇāṁ*
manuṣyānāṁ janārdana
narake'niyataṁ vāso
bhavatīty anuśuśruma

45. *aho bata mahat pāpaṁ*
kartuṁ vyavasitā vayam
yad rājya-sukha-lobhena
hantuṁ sva-janam udyatāḥ

46. *yadi mām apratīkāram*
aśastraṁ śastra-pānayaḥ
dhartarāṣṭrā raṇe hanyus
tan me kṣemataraṁ bhavet

39. We can see the evil of destroying a family. Why then, O Janardana, should we engage in such a sin?

40. With the destruction of a family, its ancient traditions are lost. When tradition is destroyed, irreligion takes over the whole family.

41. When irreligion becomes predominant women of good repute are led astray. O Varshneya, thus these women give birth to children of mixed parentage.

42. Such unplanned children bring hellish conditions to the family and to those who destroyed it, because the ancestral rites are no longer performed.

43. The evil deeds of family-destroyers create unwanted population, and traditional family religious rites are lost.

44. We have repeatedly been taught, O Janardana, that people who ruin the traditional rites of a family reside in hell.

45. Alas! We are deciding to commit a great crime and are prepared to slay our kinsmen just for the desire to enjoy royal pleasure.

46. It is better for me to be unarmed and offer no resistence to Dhritarashtra's sons and let them, with weapons in hand, slay me in the battle.

Sañjaya uvāca

47. *evam uktvārjunaḥ saṅkhye*
rathopastha upāviśat
visṛjya sa-śaraṁ cāpaṁ
śoka-saṁvigna-mānasaḥ

Sanjaya said:

47. Having thus spoken on the battlefield, Arjuna, his heart distracted with sorrow, sat down on the chariot-seat and cast aside his bow and arrows.

Chapter Two

A Summary of Bhagavad Gītā

Arjuna, as disciple, questions Lord Krishna before the battle. What follows is the highest conversation between God and man as the Supreme imparts wisdom again to the universe, paving the way with wisdom for all people to attain eternal life.

Sañjaya uvāca

1. *taṁ tathā kṛpayāviṣṭam*
aśru-pūrṇākulekṣaṇam
viṣīdantam idaṁ vākyam
uvāca madhusūdanaḥ

Śrī Bhagavān uvāca

2. *kutas tvā kaśmalam idaṁ*
viṣame samupasthitam
anārya-juṣṭam asvargyam
kīrti-karam arjuna

3. *klaibyaṁ mā sma gamaḥ pārtha*
naitat tvayy upapadyate
kṣudraṁ hṛdaya-daurbalyaṁ
tyaktvottiṣṭha parantapa

Arjuna uvāca

4. *kathaṁ bhīṣmam ahaṁ saṅkhye*
droṇaṁ ca madhusūdana
iṣubhiḥ pratiyotsyāmi
pūjārhāv ari-sūdana

5. *gurūn ahatvā hi mahānubhāvāñ*
śreyo bhoktuṁ bhaikṣyam apīha loke
hatvārtha-kāmāṁs tu gurūn ihaiva
bhuñjīya bhogān rudhirapradigdhān

6. *na caitad vidmaḥ kataran no garīyo*
yad vā jayema yadi vā no jayeyuḥ
yān eva hatvā na jijīviṣāmas
te'vasthitāḥ pramukhe dhārtarāṣṭrāḥ

Sanjaya said:

1. The despondent Arjuna was engrossed in compassion. His eyes were filled with tears. Then Krishna, slayer of the Madhu demon, spoke these words.

The Lord said:

2. How has this faint-heartedness come upon you, Arjuna? It is disgraceful and unbecoming for a nobleman. It does not lead to heaven.

3. Partha, this unmanliness is unbefitting. Give up this shameful feebleness of heart and arise, O destroyer of enemies.

Arjuna said:

4. O slayer of Madhu, slayer of foes, how can I shoot my arrows in battle at Bhishma and Drona who are worthy of honour?

5. Better to live by begging in this world than slay these men of dignity, my preceptors. Slaying these gurus, though desirous of wealth, would smear my enjoyments with blood.

6. And yet I do not know which is better, should we conquer them or they conquer us. If we slay these sons of Dhritarashtra, who stand before us, we shall not wish to live.

7. *kārpaṇya-doṣopahata-svabhāvaḥ*
pṛcchāmi tvāṁ dharma-sammūḍha-cetāḥ
yac chreyaḥ syān niścitaṁ brūhi tan me
śiṣyas te'ham śādhi māṁ tvāṁ prapannam

8. *na hi propaśyāmi mamāpanudyād*
yac chokam ucchoṣaṇam indriyāṇām
avāpya bhūmāv asapatnam ṛddham
rājyaṁ surāṇām api cādhipatyam

Sañjaya uvāca

9. *evam uktvā hṛṣīkeśaṁ*
guḍākeśaḥ paramtapah
na yotsya iti govindam
uktvā tūṣṇīṁ babhūva ha

10. *tam uvāca hṛṣīkeśaḥ*
prahasann iva bhārata
senayor ubhayor madhye
viṣīdantam idaṁ vacaḥ

Śrī Bhagavān uvāca

11. *aśocyān anvaśocas tvaṁ*
prajñā-vādāṁś ca bhāṣase
gatāsūn agatāsūṁś ca
nānuśocanti paṇḍitāḥ

12. *na tv evāhaṁ jātu nāsaṁ*
na tvaṁ neme janādhipāḥ
na caiva na bhaviṣyāmaḥ
sarve vayam ataḥ param

7. I am afflicted
   Compassion overpowers my nature
   My mind is confused
   What should be done?
   I ask You
   Tell me with certainty.
   I come to You for protection.
   I am Your disciple
   Please guide me.

8. I cannot see anything to drive away the sorrow, that withers my senses, not even the gain of an unrivalled, prosperous sovereignty on earth, or lordship over the demi-gods.

Sanjaya said:

9. Having so spoken to Krishna, Lord of the senses, Arjuna, the destroyer of enemies and conqueror of the darkness of sleep, calmed down uttering, "I shall not fight, Govinda."

10. Lord Krishna, smiling, spoke these words to a despondent Arjuna between the two armies.

The Lord said:

11. You speak words of wisdom, yet you grieve for those who should not be grieved for. The wise grieve neither for the living nor for the dead.

12. Never was there a time, when I, nor you, nor all these rulers of men did not exist, nor will there ever be a time when we shall all cease to be.

13. *dehino 'smin yathā dehe*
kaumāraṁ yauvanaṁ jarā
tathā dehāntara-prāptir
dhīras tatra na muhyati

14. *mātrā-sparśās tu kaunteya*
śītoṣṇa-sukha-duḥkha-dāḥ
āgamāpāyino 'niyās
tāṁs titikṣasva bhārata

15. *yaṁ hi na vyathayanty ete*
puruṣaṁ puruṣarṣabha
sama-duḥkha-sukhaṁ dhīram
so 'mṛtatvāya kalpate

16. *nāsato vidyate bhāvo*
nābhāvo vidyate sataḥ
ubhayor api dṛṣṭo 'ntas tv
anayos tattva-darśibhiḥ

17. *avināśi tu tad viddhi*
yena sarvam idaṁ tatam
vināśam avyayasyāsya
na kaścit kartum arhati

18. *antavanta ime dehā*
nityasyoktāḥ śarīriṇaḥ
anāśino' prameyasya
tasmād yudhyasva bhārata

19. *ya enaṁ vetti hantāraṁ*
yaś cainaṁ manyate hatam
ubhau tau na vijānīto
nāyaṁ hanti na hanyate

20. *na jāyate mriyate vā kādacin*
nāyaṁ bhūtvā bhavitā vā na bhūyaḥ
ajo nityaḥ śāśvato' yaṁ purāṇo
na hanyate hanyamāne śarīre

13. As a person changes from childhood to manhood and then to old age in this body, so he changes to another body at the time of death. The wise are not confused by this.

14. The objects which our senses come into contact with may bring joy or sorrow, heat or cold, O son of Kunti. These impressions come and go and do not last. One must learn to endure them patiently, Bharata.

15. That person who is unafflicted by all this and who is resolute and unchangeable in grief or pleasure, is fit for immortality, Arjuna.

16. The final truth is that the unreal (material body) has no wordly existence, and the real (soul) suffers no change. This has been concluded by the seers who have studied the nature of both.

17. Know, that which pervades everything is certainly imperishable. That which is imperishable, no one can destroy.

18. The material body of the eternal, indestructible and immeasurable soul is said to be perishable, Bharata. Therefore, you must fight.

19. One who thinks the soul is the slayer, or one who considers the soul as slain, are both lacking in knowledge, for the soul neither slays nor is slain.

20. Soul is never born
Soul never dies
Neither did it come into being
Nor will it ever cease to be.
Unborn, eternal, changeless, primeval
The soul is not slain
When the body is slain.

21. *vedāvināśinaṁ nityaṁ*
ya enam ajam avyayam
kathaṁ sa puruṣaḥ pārtha
kaṁ ghātayati hanti kam

22. *vāsāṁsi jīrnāni yathā vihāya*
navāni gṛhṇāti naro' parāṇi
tathā śarīrāṇi vihāya jīrṇany
anyāni saṁyāti navāni dehī

23. *nainaṁ chindanti śastrāṇi*
nainaṁ dahati pāvakaḥ
na cainaṁ kledayānty āpo
na śoṣayati mārutaḥ

24. *acchedyo' yam adāhyo' yam*
akledyo 'śoṣya eva ca
nityaḥ ṣarva-gataḥ sthāṇur
acalo' yaṁ sanātanaḥ

25. *avyakto' yam acintyo' yam*
avikāryo' yam ucyate
tasmād evaṁ viditvainaṁ
nānuśocitum arhasi

26. *atha cainaṁ nitya-jātaṁ*
nityaṁ vā manyase mṛtam
tathāpi tvaṁ mahā-bāho
nainaṁ śocitum arhasi

27. *jātasya hi dhruvo mṛtyur*
dhruvaṁ janma mṛtasya ca
tasmād aparihārye' rthe
na tvaṁ śocitum arhasi

28. *avyaktādīni bhūtāni*
vyakta-madhyāni bhārata
avyakta-nidhanāny eva
tatra kā paridevanā

21. How can a person who knows the soul to be imperishable, eternal, changeless and primeval kill or cause anyone to kill, Partha?

22. As a person casts aside worn-out garments and puts on new ones, so the soul casts aside worn-out bodies and enters new ones.

23. The soul can neither be destroyed by weapons
Nor burned by fire
Nor moistened by water
Nor desicated by wind.

24. The soul cannot be cut, burned, moistened or withered. The soul is eternal, omnipresent, fixed, immovable and ancient.

25. The soul is invisible and unchangeable.
The soul surpasses thought.
Therefore, knowing the soul in this way
You should not grieve.

26. Or, even if you think the soul is born and dies constantly, still, O mighty warrior, you should not grieve.

27. One who is born will surely die, and one who dies will surely be born. Therefore do not grieve over the unavoidable.

28. Living beings are only perceptible during a life, neither before nor after, Bharata. What cause then is there for grief?

29. *āścarya-vat paśyati kaścid enam*
āścarya-vad vadati tathaiva cānyah
āścarya-vac cainam anyaḥ śṛṇoti
śrutvāpy enaṁ veda na caiva kaścit

30. *dehī nityam avadhyo' yaṁ*
dehe sarvasya bhārata
tasmāt sarvāṇi bhūtāni
na tvaṁ śocitum arhasi

31. *sva-dharmam api cāvekṣya*
na vikampitum arhasi
dharmyād dhi yuddhāc chreyo' nyat
kṣatriyasya na vidyate

32. *yadṛcchayā copapannaṁ*
svarga-dvāram apāvṛtam
sukhinaḥ kṣatriyāḥ pārtha
labhante yuddham īdṛśam

33. *atha cet tvam imaṁ dharmyaṁ*
saṅgrāmaṁ na kariṣyasi
tataḥ sva-dharmaṁ kīrtim ca
hitvā pāpam avāpsyasi

34. *akīrtiṁ cāpi bhūtāni*
kathayiṣyanti te' vyayām
saṁbhāvitasya cākīrtir
maraṇād atiricyate

35. *bhayād raṇād uparataṁ*
maṁsyante tvāṁ mahā-rathāḥ
yeṣāṁ ca tvaṁ bahu-mato
bhūtvā yāsyasi lāghavam

36. *avācy-avādāṁś ca bahūn*
vadiṣyanti tavāhitāḥ
nindantas tava sāmarthyaṁ
tato duḥkhataraṁ nu kim

29. One person perceives the soul as marvellous
Another hears of the soul as marvellous
Another speaks of the soul as a marvel
And yet another, having heard, does not know the soul at all.

30. This soul which exists in all beings is indestructible, Bharata. Therefore you should not grieve for any being.

31. Besides, considering your own prescribed duty also, you should not waver, for there is nothing better for a warrior than a just war.

32. Members of the military order should be pleased to come across such an unexpected war, Partha. Heaven's gate is opened for them.

33. But if you will not wage this just war, forsaking your duty and fame, then you will acquire sin and loose your reputation.

34. The world will speak of your dishonour forever. And dishonour is worse than death to a honoured man.

35. Great warriors will think you withdrew from the war out of fear. The high opinion they had of you will be greatly reduced.

36. And many reproachful words will be spoken by your enemies reviling your power. What can be more agonising than that?

37. *hato vā prāpsyasi svargaṁ*
jitvā vā bhokṣyase mahīm
tasmād uttiṣṭha kaunteya
yuddhāya kṛta-niścayaḥ

38. *sukha-duḥkhe same kṛtvā*
lābhālābhau jayājayau
tato yuddhāya yujyasva
naivaṁ pāpam avāpsyasi

39. *eṣā te' bhihitā sāṅkhye*
buddhir yoge tv imāṁ śṛṇu
buddhyā yukto yayā pārtha
karma-bandhaṁ prahāsyasi

40. *nehābhikrama-nāśo' sti*
pratyavāyo na vidyate
sv-alpam apy asya dharmasya
trāyate mahato bhayāt

41. *vyavasāyātmikā buddhir-*
ekeha kuru-nandana
bahu-śakhā hy anantāś ca
buddhayo' vyavasāyinām

42. *yām imāṁ puṣpitāṁ vācaṁ*
pravadanty avipaścitaḥ
veda-vāda-ratāḥ pārtha
nānyad astīti vādinaḥ

43. *kāmātmānaḥ svarga-parā*
janma-karma-phala-pradām
kriyā-viśeṣa-bahulāṁ
bhogaiśvarya-gatiṁ prati

44. *bhogaiśvarya-prasaktānāṁ*
tayāpahṛta-cetasām
vyavasāyātmikā buddhiḥ
samādhau na vidhīyate

37. If you are slain, you will attain heaven. If you are victorious, you will inherit the earth. Rise, therefore, ready to fight with determination, son of Kunti.

38. Be ready for battle. Consider joy, sorrow, gain, loss, victory and defeat to be the same. Then you will not acquire dishonour.

39. I have spoken to you of *sankhya*-wisdom based on the philosophy of the duality of matter and soul. Now hear it in terms of *yoga*—devotional practice. By engaging in it, O Partha, you will be free from the bonds of action.

40. In devotional practice, neither is there any loss of effort nor disappointment. Even a little practice of devotion can protect one from great fear.

41. Those who are resolute in devotional practice have a single aim, O descendent of the Kurus, but the aims of those who are irresolute are varied and endless.

42-43. The ignorant, engaging in scriptural discussion, delight in the flowery words of the Vedas. Motivated by desire their goal is to attain heaven, and thus they perform many rites to achieve pleasure and power, declaring there is no other goal in life than this.

44. Those who are too attracted by pleasure and power, are bereft of intelligence, O Partha, and the firm determination for devotion does not arise in their mind.

45. *trai-guṇya-viṣayā veda*
nistrai-guṇyo bhavārjuna
nirdvandvo nitya-sattva-stho
niryoga-kṣema ātmavān

46. *yāvān artha udapāne*
sarvataḥ saṁplutodake
tāvān sarveṣu vedeṣu
brāhmaṇasya vijānataḥ

47. *karmaṇy evādhikāras te*
mā phaleṣu kadācana
mā karma-phala-hetur bhūr
mā te saṅgo' stv akarmaṇi

48. *yoga-sthaḥ kuru karmāṇi*
saṅgaṁ tyaktvā dhanañjaya
siddhy-asiddhyoḥ samo bhūtvā
samatvaṁ yoga ucyate

49. *dūreṇa hy avaraṁ karma*
buddhi-yogād dhanañjaya
buddhau śaraṇam anviccha
kṛpaṇāḥ phala-hetavaḥ

50. *buddhi-yukto jahātīha*
ubhe sukṛta-duṣkṛte
tasmād yogāya yujyasva
yogaḥ karmasu kauśalam

51. *karma-jaṁ buddhi-yuktā hi*
phalaṁ tyaktvā manīṣiṇaḥ
janma-bandha-vinirmuktāḥ
padaṁ gacchanty anāmayam

52. *yadā te moha-kalilaṁ*
buddhir vyatitariṣyati
tadā gantāsi nirvedam
śrotavyasya śrutasya ca

45. The Vedas, detail the three dominating principles of material nature, Arjuna. Transcend them. Be free from duality and the anxiety for acquisition or protection. Be steadfast in goodness and established in the self.

46. Just as a reservoir serves all the uses of a well, in the same way the Vedas contain everything for a person who is complete in knowledge.

47. You have a right to do your prescribed duty, but not to expect its fruits. Your motive should never be for the results of your actions, nor should you abstain from your prescribed duty.

48. Be absorbed in spiritual discipline Arjuna and perform your prescribed duty. Abandon attachment and be equal-minded to success or failure. Such equanimity is called *yoga.*

49. Any prescribed duty or religious act, performed in the hope of future recompense, is far inferior to intellectual union with the Supreme Spirit, Arjuna. Seek shelter in meditation. Only misers desire the results of their actions.

50. One endowed with intelligence, gives up both good and evil deeds in this world, therefore, be asorbed in *yoga. Yoga* is the art of all religious actions.

51. Sages or wise men, endowed with intelligence, give up the fruits of actions. Thus they are freed from the bondage of birth and death and reach the blissful abode.

52. When your intelligence rises above the thicket of illusion, then you will become indifferent to what sacred knowledge has taught, and will teach in the future.

53. *śruti-vipratipannā te*
yadā sthāsyati niścalā
samādhāv acalā buddhis
tadā yogam avāpsyasi

Arjuna uvāca

54. *sthita-prajñasya kā bhāsā*
samādhi-sthasya keśava
sthita-dhīḥ kiṁ prabhāṣeta
kim āsīta vrajeta kim

Śrī Bhagavān uvāca

55. *prajahāti yadā kāmān*
sarvān pārtha mano-gatān
ātmany evātmanā tuṣṭaḥ
sthita-prajñas tadocyate

56. *duḥkheṣv anudvigna-manāḥ*
sukheṣu vigata-spṛhaḥ
vīta-rāga-bhaya-krodhaḥ
sthita-dhīr munir ucyate

57. *yaḥ sarvatrānabhisnehas*
tat tat prāpya śubhāśubham
nābhinandati na dveṣṭi
tasya prajñā pratiṣṭhitā

58. *yadā saṁharate cāyaṁ*
kūrmo' ṅgānīva sarvaśaḥ
indriyāṇīndriyārthebhyas
tasya prajñā pratiṣṭhitā

59. *viṣayā vinivartante*
nirāhārasya dehinaḥ
rasa-varjaṁ raso' py asya
paraṁ dṛṣṭvā nivartate

53. When your intelligence, is not distracted by the results offered in the Vedas, and remains unwavering and firmly fixed in meditation, then you will attain *yoga.*

Arjuna said:

54. O Krishna, describe one who is firm in judgement and wisdom and who is fixed in profound meditation. How does a steady-minded person speak, rest and move about?

The Lord said:

55. When a person gives up all desires of the heart, and the mind is content in the self, then they are known to be firm in judgement and wisdom.

56. One who is devoid of desire,
Whose mind is free from anxiety, joy and sorrow,
Who is indifferent to fear and anger,
Is called the sage of steady mind.

57. One who is always undisturbed by whatever is pleasant or unpleasant that comes his way, neither delighting in nor disliking, is grounded in wisdom.

58. One who is grounded in wisdom, withdraws the senses from the sense-objects, like a tortise withdraws its limbs.

59. Sensuality comes to an end through abstinence, although desires may remain. But even those desires cease when one sees the Supreme.

60. *yatato hy api kaunteya*
puruṣasya vipaścitaḥ
indriyāṇi pramāthīni
haranti prasabhaṁ manaḥ

61. *tāni sarvāni saṁyamya*
yukta āsīta mat-paraḥ
vaśe hi yasyendriyāṇi
tasya prajñā pratiṣṭhitā

62 *dhyāyato viṣayān puṁsaḥ*
saṅgas teṣūpajāyate
saṅgāt sañjāyate kāmaḥ
kāmāt krodho' bhijāyate

63. *krodhād bhavati sammohaḥ*
sammohāt smṛti-vibhramaḥ
smṛti-bhraṁśād buddi-nāśo
budhi-nāśāt praṇaśyati

64. *rāga-dveṣa-vimuktais tu*
viṣayān indriyaiś caran
ātma-vaśyair vidheyātmā
prasādam adhigacchati

65. *pasāde sarva-duḥkhānāṁ*
hānir asyopajāyate
prasanna-cetaso hy āśu
buddhiḥ paryavatiṣṭhate

66. *nāsti buddhir ayuktasya*
na cāyutasya bhāvanā
na cābhāvayataḥ śāntir
aśāntasya kutaḥ sukham

67. *indriyāṇāṁ hi caratāṁ*
yan mano' nuvidhīyate
tad asya harati prajñāṁ
vāyur nāvam ivāmbhasi

60. The senses are so tormenting, Arjuna, that they can forcibly carry away the mind of even an inspired person who is striving after perfection.

61. One should sit down, with all the senses under control, and concentrate on Me. One who controls the senses is indeed grounded in wisdom.

62. One who contemplates sensuality becomes attached. From such attachment desire arises, and from desire anger arises.

63. From anger illusion arises
From illusion, confusion of the mind
From such confusion, loss of intelligence
And from loss of intelligence, a person perishes.

64. But when a person is self-restrained in the world, bringing his senses under control, free from attraction and hatred, he receives God's grace.

65. In God's grace all calamities are quelled, for the intelligence of a tranquil-minded person is well established in divine consciousness.

66. Without devotion there is no wisdom. One who does not meditate can find no peace. Without peace, how can there be happiness?

67. As the wind carries away a boat on the water, the mind that yields to the wandering senses carries away one's wisdom.

68. *tasmād yasya mahā-bāho*
nigṛhītāni sarvaśaḥ
indriyāṇīndriyārthebhyas
tasya prajñā pratiṣṭhitā

69. *yā niśā sarva-bhūtānāṁ*
tasyāṁ jāgarti saṁyamī
yasyām jāgrati bhūtāni
sā niśā paśyato muneḥ

70. *āpūryamāṇam acala-pratiṣṭhaṁ*
samudram āpaḥ praviśanti yadvat
tadvat kāmā yaṁ praviśanti sarve
sa śāntim āpnoti na kāma-kāmī

71. *vihāya kāmān yaḥ sarvān*
pumāṃś carati niḥspṛhaḥ
nirmamo nirahaṅkāraḥ
sa śāntim adhigacchati

72. *eṣā brāhmī sthitiḥ pārtha*
nainaṁ prāpya vimuhyati
sthitvāsyām anta-kāle' pi
brahma-nirvāṇamṛcchati

68. Therefore, O mighty warrior, one whose senses are wholly restrained from the world of senses, is one who is firmly rooted in wisdom.

69. A person of self-control is awake in what is night for all living beings. What is day for all living beings, is night for the meditative sage.

70. As the ocean remains undisturbed as the rivers flow into it, so a person can only find peace if he experiences the flow of desires without seeking to fulfil them.

71. That humble person who lives having abandoned all desires, and is devoid of all worldly connections, obtains peace.

72. This is the divine state, Partha. Attaining this, no one is deluded. Abiding in it, even at death, one obtains absorption into the One self-existent Spirit.

CHAPTER THREE

The *Yoga* of Action

The Lord describes two paths, that of philosophical knowledge and that of action. Since all people are obliged to act according to their natural qualities, Krishna recommends action to be performed for the pleasure of the Lord, without attachment. The real enemies of mankind are desire and anger.

Arjuna uvāca

1. *jyāyasī cet karmaṇas te*
matā buddhir janārdana
tat kiṁ karmaṇi ghore māṁ
niyojayasi keśava

2. *vyāmiśreṇeva vākyena*
buddhiṁ mohayasīva me
tad ekaṁ vada niścitya
yena śreyo' ham āpnuyām

Śrī Bhagavān uvāca

3. *loke' smin dvi-vidhā niṣṭhā*
purā proktā mayānagha
jñāna-yogena sāṅkhyānāṁ
karma-yogena yogināṁ

4. *na karmaṇām anārambhān*
naiṣkarmyaṁ puruso' śnute
na ca sannyasanād eva
siddhiṁ samadhigacchati

5. *na hi kaścit kṣaṇam api*
jātu tiṣṭhaty akarma-kṛt
kāryate hy avaśaḥ karma
sarvaḥ prakṛti-jair guṇaiḥ

6. *karmendriyāṇi saṁyamya*
ya āste manasā smaran
indriyārthān vimūḍhātmā
mithyācāraḥ sa ucyate

7. *yas tv indriyāṇi manasā*
niyamyārabhate' rjuna
karmendriyaiḥ karma-yogam
asaktaḥ sa viśiṣyate

Arjuna said:

1. O Janardana, if You say, intelligence, is superior to action, why then do You urge me on the course of this dreadful action, O Kesava?

2. Your intricate words confuse me. Please tell me the one thing for certain by which I can attain the bliss of final emancipation.

The Lord said:

3. O guiltless Arjuna, previously I taught the two-fold path to the world. For the adherents of *sankhya* doctrine I taught the path of philosophical knowledge, and for the yogis—devotees–the path of religious duties.

4. A person, neither reaches inactivity by abstaining from religious duties, nor gains final emancipation by renouncing the world alone.

5. Since we are born of nature, no one ever remains inactive, even for a moment. Everybody is obliged to be active due to their material qualities.

6. A person who restrains the sense-organs, but lets his mind dwell on sense objects, is known as foolish and a hypocrite.

7. But, whoever controls the senses with his mind, and clings to religious duties with determination and detachment, is far better, Arjuna.

8. *niyataṁ kuru karma tvaṁ*
karma jyāyo hy akarmaṇaḥ
śarīra-yātrapi ca te
na prasidhyed akarmaṇaḥ

9. *yajñārthāt karmaṇo' nyatra*
loko' yaṁ karma-bandhanaḥ
tad-arthaṁ karma kaunteya
mukta-sangaḥ samācara

10. *saha-yajñāḥ prajāḥ sṛṣṭvā*
purovāca prajāpatiḥ
anena prasaviṣyadhvam
eṣa vo' stviṣṭa-kāma-dhuk

11. *devān bhāvayatānena*
te devā bhāvayantu vaḥ
parasparaṁ bhavayantaḥ
śreyaḥ param avāpsyatha

12. *iṣṭān bhogān hi va devā*
dāsyante yajña-bhāvitāḥ
tair dattān apradāyaibhyo
yo bhuṅkte stena eva saḥ

13. *yajña-śiṣṭāśinaḥ santo*
mucyante sarva-kilbiṣaiḥ
bhuñjate te tv aghaṁ pāpā
ye pacanty ātma-kāraṇāt

14. *annād bhavanti bhūtāni*
parjanyād anna-sambhavaḥ
yajñād bhavati parjanyo
yajñāḥ karma-samāudbhavaḥ

15. *karma brahmodbhavaṁ viddhi*
brahmākṣara-samudbhavam
tasmāt sarva-gataṁ braham
nityaṁ yajñe pratiṣṭhitam

8. Perform your religious duties, for action is better than inaction. Besides, inaction is unsuitable for the maintenance of one's body.

9. Work in this world is bound by actions and consequences, except that which is dedicated to Lord Vishnu. Therefore, Kaunteya, perform your religious duties free from attachment, for the pleasure of the Lord.

10. Long ago, God created mankind together with sacrifice. He said, "Let this sacrifice bring you the fulfilment of all your desires."

11. By pleasing the demigods with sacrifice they will protect you. And by pleasing each other, you shall attain supreme bliss.

12. Being pleased by sacrifice, the demigods will surely grant your desires. But whoever enjoys what is given by them, offering nothing in return, is truly a thief.

13. The devotees eat the remnants of sacrifices by which they are freed from sin. But the sceptics, who cook only for their own enjoyment, eat food that is impure.

14. Food maintains all living beings. And is produced by rain. Sacrifice invokes the rain and is performed out of duty.

15. Know, religious rites come from *brahman*, the impersonal Spirit. *Brahman* is created by the imperishable Lord. Omnipresent *brahman* is therefore eternally established in sacrifice.

16. *evaṁ pravartitaṁ cakraṁ*
nānuvartayatīha yaḥ
aghāyur indriyārāmo
moghaṁ pārtha sa jīvati

17. *yas tv ātma-ratir eva syād*
ātma-tṛptaś ca mānavaḥ
ātmany eva ca santuṣṭas
tasya kāryaṁ na vidyate

18. *naiva tasya kṛtenārtho*
nākṛteneha kaścana
na cāsya sarva-bhūteṣu
kaścid artha-vyapāśrayaḥ

19. *tasmād asaktaḥ satataṁ*
kāryaṁ karma samācara
asakto hy ācaran karma
param āpnoti pūruṣaḥ

20. *karmaṇaiva hi saṁsiddhim*
āsthitā janakadayah
loka-saṅgraham evāpi
sampaśyan kartum arhasi

21. *yad yad ācarati śreṣṭhas*
tat tad evetaro janaḥ
sa yat pramāṇaṁ kurute
lokas tad anuvartate

22. *na me pārthāsti kartavyaṁ*
triṣu lokeṣu kiñcana
nānavāptam avāptavyaṁ
varta eva ca karmaṇi

23. *yadi hy ahaṁ na varteyaṁ*
jātu karmaṇy atandritaḥ
mama vartmānuvartante
manuṣyāḥ pārtha sarvaśaḥ

16. Whoever does not follow this cycle of phenomena as established in this world, lives in sin, Partha. He delights in the senses and his life is in vain.

17. But the person who rejoices in the Supreme Spirit, is satisfied in the Supreme Spirit, is truly content in the Supreme Spirit, for them, there is no need for action.

18. For them action or inaction serves no purpose. They are only dependent on the self, and have no need to rely on anybody for anything.

19. Therefore, always do your required duty free from attachment. Duty done in this way surely leads one to the Supreme.

20. By perfomance of such religious rites, King Janaka and others attained perfection. As you are concerned with the welfare of the world, so you should also act.

21. Whatever an honourable man does, others surely follow. The standards which he establishes for himself, are pursued by the world.

22. There is nothing I have to do or attain in the three worlds O Arjuna, yet I engage Myself in action.

23. For if I did not engage Myself assiduously in action, humanity everywhere would follow My path.

24. *utsīdeyur ime lokā*
na kuryāṁ karma ced aham
saṁkarasya ca kartā syām
upahanyām imāḥ prajāḥ

25. *saktāḥ karmaṇy avidvāṁso*
yathā kurvanti bhārata
kuryād vidvāṁs tathāsaktaś
cikīrṣur loka-saṅgraham

26. *na buddhi-bhedaṁ janayed*
ajñānāṁ karma-saṅginām
joṣayet sarva-karmāṇi
vidvān yuktaḥ samācaran

27. *prakrteḥ kriyamāṇāni*
guṇaih karmāṇi sarvaśaḥ
ahaṅkāra-vimūḍhātmā
kartāham iti manyate

28. *tattva-vit tu mahā-bāho*
guṇa-karma-vibhāgayoḥ
guṇā guṇeṣu vartanta
iti matvā na sajjate

29. *prakṛter guṇa-sammūḍhāḥ*
sajjante guṇa-karmasu
tān akṛtsna-vido mandān
kṛtsna-vin na vicālayet

3. *mayi sarvāṇi karmani*
sannyasyādhyātma-cetasā
nirāśīr nirmamo bhūtvā
yudhyasva vigata-jvaraḥ

31. *ye me matam idaṁ nityam*
anutiṣṭhanti mānavāḥ
śraddhāvanto' nasūyanto
mucyante te' pi karmabhiḥ

24. If I did no action, these worlds would fall into ruin. I would be the cause of unwanted population, and I would destroy these people.

25. The ignorant do their duties with attachment, Bharata. The wise should also perform their duties, but without attachment, intent on the welfare of the world.

26. Although the ignorant do their duties with attachment, their minds must not be disturbed. The wise devotee should engage others in all the activities that he does in a spirit of devotion.

27. All acts are universally performed by the dominating principles of material nature—*gunas.* One whose mind is perplexed by egoism thinks, "I am the doer."

28. But the knower of truth, O mighty warrior, can distinguish an action and an attribute. He remains free from them, for he knows how the senses and sense-objects, pertaining to the *gunas,* affect one another.

29. Deluded by the attributes of this material world, ignorant people attach themselves to unspiritual activities. However, the spiritually wise should never disturb those of incomplete knowledge.

30. Meditate on Me.
Entrust all your actions to Me.
Be free from expectation,
From all worldly connections and morbid feelings.
Fight Arjuna!

31. Those people who continually attend to My teaching, full of faith and goodwill, are released from their actions also.

32. *ye tv etad abhyasūyanto*
nanutiṣṭhanti me matam
sarva jñāna-vimūḍhāṁs tān
viddhi naṣṭān acetasaḥ

33. *sadṛśaṁ ceṣṭate svasyāḥ*
prakṛter jñānavān api
prakṛtiṁ yānti bhūtāni
nigrahaḥ kiṁ kariṣyati

34. *indriyasyendriyasyārthe*
rāga-dveṣau, vyavasthitau
tayor na vaśam āgacchet
tau hy asya paripanthinau

35. *śreyān sva-dharmo viguṇaḥ*
para-dharmāt sv-anuṣṭhitāt
sva-dharme nidhanaṁ śreyaḥ
para-dharmo bhayāvahaḥ

Arjuna uvāca

36. *atha kena prayukto' yaṁ*
pāpaṁ carati pūruṣaḥ
anicchann api vārṣṇeya
balād iva niyojitaḥ

Śrī Bhagavan uvāca

37. *kāma eṣa krodha eṣa*
rajo-guṇa-samudbhavaḥ
mahāśano mahā-pāpmā
viddhy enam iha vairiṇam

38. *dhūmenāvriyate vahnir*
yathādarśo malena ca
yatholbenāvṛto garbhas
tathā tenedam āvṛtam

32. But those who are indignant at My teaching and do not attend to it, are foolish and insensible. Know that they are lost.

33. Even a person of spiritual knowledge acts according to his own nature. All living beings are led by their nature. What can restraint accomplish?

34. For the senses, there exist in their objects, both love and hatred. A person should not come under the control of love and hatred. They are enemies.

35. It is better to do one's own prescribed duty imperfectly rather than do someone else's perfectly. Death in the course of one's own prescribed duty, is better than the danger of following someone else's duty.

Arjuna said:

36. Then what leads a person, as if by force, unwillingly into sin, son of Vrishni?

The Lord said:

37 It is desire and anger. They arise from the principle of passion. They are voracious and do much evil. Know that they are enemies of this world.

38. As smoke conceals fire, dust clouds a mirror, and a membrane envelopes the embryo, so this enemy lust envelopes the world.

39. *āvṛtaṁ jñānam etena*
jñānino nitya-vairiṇā
kāma-rūpeṇa kaunteya
duṣpūreṇanālena ca

40. *indriyāṇi mano buddhir*
asyādhiṣṭhānam ucyate
etair vimohayaty eṣa
jñānam āvṛtya dehinam

41. *tasmāt tvam indriyāṇy ādau*
niyamya bharatarṣabha
pāpmānaṁ prajahi hy enaṁ
jñāna-vijñā-nāśanam

42. *indriyāṇi parāṇy āhur*
indriyebhyaḥ paraṁ manaḥ
manasas tu parā buddhir
yo buddheḥ paratas tu saḥ

43. *evaṁ buddheḥ paraṁ buddhvā*
saṁstabhyātmānam ātmanā
jahi śatruṁ mahā-bāho
kāma-rūpaṁ durāsadam

39. These persistent enemies of the wise veil wisdom, O Kaunteya. They are like a never-quenched fire of desire.

40. These enemies reside in the senses, the mind and the intellect. Through them, these enemies veil wisdom and delude humanity.

41. Therefore, O Prince, first subdue the senses, then slay this destroyer of sacred wisdom and doctrine.

42. It is said that the senses are higher than matter, but the mind is higher than the senses. Intelligence is higher than the mind. Yet that which is higher than intelligence, is the soul.

43. Therefore, knowing the soul to be above the intelligence, mighty warrior, strengthen your mind by your higher self and conquer desire, this formidable enemy.

Chapter Four

The Highest Mystery

Krishna describes the history of Bhagavad Gītā and how He descends Himself periodically to re-establish its message. There are four divisions of human nature with activities prescribed for each which free one from the laws of karma.

Śrī Bhagavan uvāca

1. *imaṁ vivasate yogaṁ*
proktavān aham avyayam
vivasvān manave prāha
manur ikṣvākave' bravīt

2. *evaṁ paramparā-prāptam*
imaṁ rājarṣayo vidhuḥ
sa kāleneha mahatā
yogo naṣṭaḥ paramtapa

3. *sa evāyaṁ mayā te' dya*
yogaḥ proktaḥ purātanaḥ
bhakto' si me sakhā ceti
rahasyaṁ hy etad uttamam

Arjuna uvāca

4. *aparaṁ bhavato janma*
paraṁ janma vivasvataḥ
katham etad vijānīyām
tvam ādau proktavān iti

Śrī Bhagavān uvāca

5. *bahūni me vyatītāni*
janmāni tava cārjuna
tāny ahaṁ veda sarvani
na tvaṁ vettha parantapa

6. *ajo' pi sann avyayatma*
bhutanam iśvaro' pi san
prakṛtiṁ svām adhiṣṭhāya
sambhavāmy ātma-māyayā

7. *yadā yadā hi dharmasya*
glānir bhavati bhārata
abhyutthānam adharmasya
tadātmānaṁ sṛjāmy aham

The Lord said:

1. I declared this imperishable *yoga* to Vivasvan, the sun-god. Vivasvan taught it to Manu, father of the human race. Manu imparted it to his son Ikshvaku.

2. This *yoga* was given in succession to the saintly kings and understood by them. But after a long laspe of time in this world, it was lost.

3. Because you are my devotee and friend I am teaching you today this same *yoga* which I taught in ancient times. This is indeed the highest mystery.

Arjuna said:

4. By birth Vivasvan is senior to You. How am I to understand that You originally taught this mystery to him?

The Lord said:

5. You and I have taken many births, Arjuna. I remember all of them, but you do not.

6. Although I am imperishable, eternally existing, and Lord of all beings, I still appear in this material world by Myself.

7. Whenever the spiritual principles decline and there is a rise of whimsicality, at that time I manifest Myself, Bharata.

8. *paritrāṇāya sādhūnāṁ*
vināśāya ca duṣkṛtām
dharma-saṁsthāpanārthāya
sambhavāmi yuge yuge

9. *janma karma ca me divyam*
evaṁ yo vetti tattvataḥ
tyaktvā dehaṁ punar janma
naiti mām eti so' rjuna

10. *vīta-rāga-bhayā-krodhā*
man-mayā mām upāśritāḥ
bahavo jñāna-tapasā
pūtā mad-bhāvam āgatāḥ

11. *ye yathā māṁ prapadyante*
tāṁs tathaiva bhajāmy aham
mama vartmānuvartante
manuṣyāḥ pārtha sarvaśaḥ

12. *kāṅkṣantaḥ karmaṇāṁ siddhiṁ*
yajanta iha devatāḥ
kṣipraṁ hi mānuṣe loke
siddhir bhavati karma-jā

13. *cātur-varṇyaṁ mayā sṛṣṭaṁ*
guṇa-karma-vibhāgaśaḥ
tasya kartāram api māṁ
viddhy akartāram avyayam

14. *na māṁ karmāṇi limpanti*
na me karma-phale spṛhā
iti māṁ yo' bhijānāti
karmabhir na sa badhyate

15. *evaṁ jñātvā kṛtaṁ karma*
pūrvair api mumukṣubhiḥ
kuru karmaiva tasmāt tvaṁ
pūrvaiḥ pūrvataraṁ kṛtam

8. I incarnate, age after age
   To preserve the virtuous,
   To destroy the vicious,
   And to re-establish spiritual principles.

9. One who, in reality, knows My supernatural birth and activities, after leaving this material body, is not reborn, but comes to Me, Arjuna.

10. Freed from attachment, fear and anger, absorbed in Me, relying on Me, purified by austerity and wisdom, many people have attained My intrinsic nature.

11. As people take refuge in Me, so I grant them grace. Everyone follows My path in every respect, Partha.

12. In this world, people desire success for their activities, and so they worship and offer sacrifices to the demi-gods, and success comes quickly indeed.

13. I created the four divisions of society according to their qualities and actions. But, although I created this, know that I am changeless and perform no actions.

14. Actions do not affect Me, nor do I desire the fruits of action. One who recognises this of Me, is not bound by his actions.

15. Knowing Me thus, the seekers of liberation in ancient days did their duty. Therefore, do your duty too as they did in ancient times.

16. *kiṁ karma kim akarmeti*
kavayo' py atra mohitāḥ
tat te karma pravakṣyāmi
yaj jñātvā mokṣyase' śubhāt

17. *karmaṇo hy api boddhavyaṁ*
boddhavyaṁ ca vikarmaṇaḥ
akarmaṇaś ca boddhavyaṁ
gahanā karmaṇo gatiḥ

18. *karmaṇy akarma yaḥ paśyed*
akarmaṇi ca karma yaḥ
sa buddhimān manuṣyeṣu
sa yuktaḥ kṛtsna-karma-kṛt

19. *yasya sarve samārambhāḥ*
kāma-saṅkalpa-varjitāḥ
jñānāgni-dagdha-karmāṇaṁ
tam āhuḥ paṇḍitaṁ budhāḥ

20. *tyaktvā karma-phalāsaṅgaṁ*
nitya-tṛpto nirāśrayaḥ
karmaṇy abhipravṛtto' pi
naiva kiṁcit karoti saḥ

21. *nirāśīr yata-cittātmā*
tyakta-sarva-parigrahaḥ
śārīraṁ kevalaṁ karma
kurvan nāpnoti kilbiṣam

22. *yadṛcchā-lābha-santuṣṭo*
dvandvātīto vimatsaraḥ
samaḥ siddhāv asiddhau ca
kṛtvāpi na nibadhyate

23. *gata-saṅgasya muktasya*
jñānāvasthita-cetasaḥ
yajñāyācarataḥ karma
samagraṁ pravilīyate

16. Even the wise get confused with what is action and what is inaction. I shall, therefore, teach you what action is. Knowing this will free you from misfortune.

17. One should know what is proper action. One should also know what prohibited action is. And one should know what is inaction. It is very difficult to understand the course of action.

18. Whoever sees inaction in action and action in inaction is wise among people. He is a true ascetic and performs proper actions.

19. The person whose undertakings are devoid of all desires and whose actions are consumed by the fire of knowledge, is called wise by the sages.

20. Having abandoned all desires for the fruits of action, always content and self-sufficient, although engaged in action, he really does nothing.

21. Without desires, without sense of ownership, with mind and body under control, performing mere works to maintain the body, he incurs no sin.

22. Free from envy
Free from duality
Content with obtaining what comes spontaneously
Equal towards success and failure
Though he acts, his acts do not bind him.

23. Free from attachment
Liberated from sin
With mind and heart absorbed in knowledge
Engaged in spiritual devotion
His actions melt away.

24. *brahmārpaṇaṁ brahma haviṛ*
brahmāgnau brahmaṇā hutam
brahmaiva tena gantavyam
brahma-karma-samādhinā

25. *daivam evāpare yajñaṁ*
yoginaḥ paryupāsate
brahmāgnāv apare yajñaṁ
yajñenaivopajuhvati

26. *śrotrādīnīndriyāṇy anye*
saṁyamāgniṣu juhvati
śabdādīn viṣayān anya
indriyāgniṣu juhvati

27. *sarvāṇīndriya-karmāṇi*
prāṇa-karmāṇi cāpare
ātma-saṁyama-yogāgnau
juhvati jñāna-dīpite

28. *dravya-yajñās tapo-yajñā*
yoga-yajñās tathāpare
svādhyāya-jñāna-yajñāś ca
yatayaḥ saṁśita-vratāḥ

29. *apāne juhvati prānaṁ*
prāṇe' pānaṁ tathāpare
prāṇāpana-gatī-ruddhvā
prāṇāyāma-parāyaṇāḥ

30. *apare niyatāhārāḥ*
prāṇān prāṇeṣu juhvati
sarve' py ete yajña-vido
yajña-kṣapita-kalmaṣāḥ

31. *yajña-śiṣṭāmṛta-bhujo*
yānti brahma sanātanam
nāyaṁ loko' sty ayajñasya
kuto' nyaḥ kuru-sattama

24. That which is offered in the sacred texts, is *brahman.* The sacrificial butter itself is *brahman.* That which is offered in sacrifice is of the same spiritual nature as he who makes the offering. One who is absorbed in this awareness shall indeed attain their spiritual destiny.

25. Some devotees only worship the demi-gods, making offerings to them. Others, offer their devotion as an oblation in the fire of *brahman.*

26. Some offer the sense of hearing in the fire of restraint. Others offer the objects of wordly desires, such as sound, in the fire of sacrifice.

27. Some offer all the senses of actions, all the vital functions of life, in the fire of the *yoga* of sense-control, illuminated by wisdom.

28. Likewise, there are others who offer wealth, austerity and y*oga* as sacrifice. The devotees, who have taken to strict vows, sacrifice in the study of the Vedas.

29. Others offer the outgoing life-breath in the incoming, and the incoming in the outgoing, as sacrifice. They restrain the movement of the air they breathe in and breathe out and thus are established in breath control.

30. Others, restraining from food, offer nothing but the life-breath itself as sacrifice. All these performers are skilled in sacrifice and their sins are washed away.

31. Those who taste the remnants of sacrifice, go to the eternal *brahman.* O Arjuna, there can be no happiness in this world, nor the next, for one who does no sacrifice.

32. *evaṁ bahu-vidhā yajñā*
vitatā brahmaṇo mukhe
karma-jān viddhi tān sarvān
evaṁ jñātvā vimokṣyase

33. *śreyān dravya-mayād yajñāj*
jñāna-yajñaḥ parantapa
sarvaṁ karmākhilaṁ pārtha
jñāne parisamāpyate

34. *tad viddhi praṇipātena*
paripraśnena sevayā
upadekṣyanti te jñānaṁ
jñāninas tattva-darśinaḥ

35. *yaj jñātvā na punar moham*
evaṁ yāsyasi pāṇḍava
yena bhūtāny aśeṣaṇa
drakṣyasy ātmany atho mayi

36. *api ced asi pāpebhyaḥ*
sarvebhyah pāpa-kṛt-tamaḥ
sarvam jñāna-plavenaiva
vṛjinaṁ samtariṣyasi

37. *yathaidhāṁsi samiddho' gnir*
bhasma-sat kurute' rjuna
jñānāgniḥ sarva-karmāṇi
bhasma-sāt kurute tathā

38. *na hi jñānena sadṛśaṁ*
pavitram iha vidyate
tat svayaṁ yoga-samsiddhaḥ
kālenātmani vindati

39. *śraddhāvāl labhate jñānaṁ*
tat-paraḥ saṁyatendriyaḥ
jñānaṁ labdhvā parāṁ śāntim
acireṇādhigacchati

32. Thus various sacrifices are unfolded in the Vedas. Know them to be born of different kinds of work, for knowing them as such, you will be freed.

33. Sacrifice performed in knowledge is better than the sacrifice of wealth, O destroyer of enemies. All religious acts, in essence, end in knowledge, Partha.

34. The wise, who have seen the truth will teach you. Submit yourself to them. Learn that truth by asking questions and by devotion.

35. When you have learned the truth, O descendent of Pandu, you will not be confused thus again. By this you will see that all living beings exist in the Supreme Soul, and are Mine.

36. Even if you are the worst of all evildoers, you will cross over the ocean of distress on the boat of this knowledge.

37. As fire reduces firewood to ashes, so does the fire of knowledge burn to ashes the results of all bad actions.

38. There is no purifier like knowledge in this world. One who becomes perfected in *yoga*, finds knowledge within himself in due course of time.

39. One with steady faith, who is devoted and controls his senses, gains knowledge. Having gained knowledge, he soon finds the highest peace.

40. *ajñaś cāśraddadhānaś ca*
saṁśayātmā vinaśyati
nāyaṁ loko' sti na paro
na sukhaṁ saṁśayātmanaḥ

41. *yoga-samnyasta-karmāṇaṁ*
jñāna-sañchinna-saṁśayam
ātmavantaṁ na karmāṇi
nibadhnanti dhanañjaya

42. *tasmād ajñāna-sambhūtaṁ*
hṛt-sthaṁ jñānāsinātmanaḥ
chittvainaṁ saṁśayaṁ yogam
ātiṣṭhottiṣṭha bhārata

40. The ignorant, the faithless and the sceptic perish. The sceptic has neither happiness in this world nor the next.

41. The self-possessed, who practises spiritual discipline unattached to the fruits thereof, and whose doubts are dispelled by knowledge, is not bound by actions.

42. Therefore, with the sword of knowledge, dispel this doubt born of ignorance which is in your heart. Submit to *yoga* Bharata. Arise!

CHAPTER FIVE

Renunciation of the Fruits of Action

By performing religious acts the ascetic achieves spiritual understanding in this world, and peace and absorption in God.

Arjuna uvāca

1. *samnyāsaṁ karmaṇāṁ kṛṣṇa*
punar yogaṁ ca śaṁsasi
yac chreya etayor ekam
tan me brūhi su-niścitam

Śrī Bhagavan uvāca

2. *samnyāsaḥ karma-yogaś ca*
niḥśreyasa-karāv ubhau
tayos tu karma-samnyāsāt
karma-yogo viśiṣyate

3. *jñeyaḥ sa nitya-samnyāsī*
yo na dveṣṭi na kāṅkṣati
nirdvandvo hi mahā-bāho
sukhaṁ bandhāt pramucyate

4. *sāṅkhya-yogau pṛthag bālāḥ*
pravadanti na paṇḍitāḥ
ekam apy āsthitaḥ samyag
ubhayor vindate phalam

5. *yat sāṅkhyaiḥ prāpyate sthānaṁ*
tad yogair api gamyate
ekaṁ sāṅkhyaṁ ca yogaṁ ca
yaḥ paśyati sa paśyati

6. *sannyāsas tu mahā-bāho*
duḥkham āptum ayogataḥ
yoga-yukto munir brahma
na cireṇādhigacchati

7. *yoga-yukto viśuddhātmā*
vijitātmā jitendriyaḥ
sarva-bhūtātma-bhūtātmā
kurvann api na lipyate

Arjuna said:

1. O Krishna, You praise the renunciation of action and also the performance of religious activity. Tell me for certain which of the two is better?

The Lord said:

2. Renunciation of action and the performance of religious activity both lead to ultimate bliss, but the performance of religious activity excels the renunciation of action.

3. It should be known, mighty Arjuna, a confirmed ascetic, who neither desires nor despises, and who is indifferent to duality, is easily liberated from material bondage.

4. The ignorant speak of devotional activity and knowledge as separate, but not the wise. Being established in one, a person gains the fruit of both.

5. Analytical knowledge and devotional *yoga* lead to the same state. One who perceives analytical knowledge and devotional activities as one, actually sees.

6. Renunciation is difficult to attain without devotion, Arjuna. The sage, immersed in devotional activities, soon reaches God.

7. Pure in mind
Self-controlled
With subdued senses
Immersed in the *yoga* of devotion
And faithful to all beings
Such a person, even when he acts, is not enmeshed.

8. *naiva kiñcit karomīti*
yukto manyeta tattva-vit
paśyañ śṛṇvan spṛśañ jighrann
aśnan gacchan svapaṇ śvasan

9. *pralapan visṛjan gṛhṇann*
unmiṣan nimiṣann api
indriyāṇīndriyārtheṣu
vartanta iti dhārayan

10. *brahmaṇy ādhāya karmāṇi*
saṅgaṁ tyaktvā karoti yaḥ
lipyate na sa pāpena
padma-patram ivāmbhasā

11. *kāyena manasā buddhyā*
kevalair indriyair api
yoginaḥ karma kurvanti
saṅgaṁ tyaktvātma-śuddhaye

12. *yuktaḥ karma-phalaṁ tyaktvā*
śāntim āpnoti naiṣṭhikīn
ayuktaḥ kāma-kāreṇa
phale sakto nibadhyate

13. *sarva-karmāṇi manasā*
sannyasyāste sukhaṁ vaśī
nava-dvāre pure dehī
naiva kurvan na kārayan

14. *na kartṛtvaṁ na karmāṇi*
lokasya sṛjati prabhuḥ
na karma-phala-saṁyogaṁ
svabhāvas tu pravartate

15. *nādatte kasyacit pāpaṁ*
na caiva sukṛtaṁ vibhuḥ
ajñānenāvṛtaṁ jñānaṁ
tena muhyanti jantavaḥ

8-9. The knower of the Truth, immersed in devotion, believes that he does nothing, although he sees, hears, touches, smells, eats, sleeps, evacuates, opens and shuts his eyes. He knows it is but the play of the senses with the sense-objects.

10. One who acts in devotion for God, forsaking worldly attachment, is not touched by sin, as the lotus leaf is not touched by water.

11. The ascetic, having given up wordly attachment, performs activities with body, mind, intelligence and the senses, only for self-purification.

12. The ascetic, renouncing the fruit of his activities, attains ultimate peace, whereas the sceptic tries to fulfil his desires and cling to the fruit. He therefore becomes enchained.

13. Mentally renouncing all acts, the person of self-control dwells happily in the city of nine gates—the body—neither acting nor causing actions to occur.

14. Neither acts, nor actions, nor attachment to the fruits of actions are created for this world by God. They are carried out by material nature.

15. The Lord does not take on Himself the good or evil actions of anyone. Ignorance veils wisdom and bewilders people.

16. *jñānena tu tad ajñānaṁ*
yeṣāṁ nāśitam ātmanaḥ
teṣām āditya-vaj jñānaṁ
prakāśayati tat param

17. *tad-buddhayas tad-ātmānas*
tan-niṣṭhās tat-parāyaṇāḥ
gacchanty apunar-āvṛttiṁ
jñāna-nirdhūta-kalmaṣāḥ

18. *vidyā-vinaya-sampanne*
brāhmaṇe gavi hastini
śuni caiva śva-pāke ca
paṇḍitāḥ sama-darśinaḥ

19. *ihai va tair jitaḥ sargo*
yeṣāṁ sāmye sthitaṁ manaḥ
nirdoṣam hi samam brahma
tasmād brahmaṇi te sthitāḥ

20. *na prahṛṣyet priyaṁ prāpya*
no dvijet prāpya cāpriyam
sthira-buddhir asammūḍho
brahma-vid brahmaṇi sthitaḥ

21. *bāhya-sparśeṣv asaktātmā*
vindaty ātmani yat sukham
sa brahma-yoga-yuktātmā
sukham akṣayam aśnute

22. *ye hi saṁsparśa-jā bhogā*
duḥkha-yonaya eva te
ādy-antavantaḥ kaunteya
na teṣu ramate budhaḥ

23. *śaknotīhaiva yaḥ soḍhuṁ*
prāk śarīra-vimokṣaṇāt
kāma-krodhodbhavaṁ vegaṁ
sa yuktaḥ sa sukhī naraḥ

16. But when knowledge of the self destroys that ignorance, then knowledge, like the sun, reveals what is the highest truth.

17. When one's mind and soul are fixed in God
When one has faith and takes shelter in God
When one is conscious of God
Then knowledge washes away one's doubts
And one reaches freedom from rebirth.

18. One who is endowed with knowledge, looks impartially on a person of divine understanding, a cow, an elephant, a dog, a scholar or an outcaste.

19. Even in this life, those whose minds are established in equanimity, have overcome the world of birth and death. Since *brahman* is infallible and is merged in equanimity, so they rest on *brahman.*

20. Undeluded and steady-minded, the knower of God, established in God, neither rejoices at something pleasant, nor laments over something unpleasant.

21. With the mind detached from external contacts, one finds happiness in oneself. Wholly intent upon devotional practice, one reaches eternal bliss.

22. Pleasures derived from sense contact are only sources of misery, they have a beginning and an end, son of Kunti. A wise person takes no delight in them.

23. One who can, before death, resist agitation born of desire and anger, is a God-centred and contented person.

24. *yo' ntaḥ-sukho' ntar-ārāmas*
tathāntar-jyotir eva yaḥ
so yogī brahma-nirvāṇaṁ
brahma-bhūto' dhigacchati

25. *labhante brahma-nirvāṇam*
ṛṣayaḥ kṣīṇa-kalmaṣāḥ
chinna-dvaidhā yatātmānaḥ
sarva-bhūta-hite ratāḥ

26. *kāma-krodha-vimuktānāṁ*
yatīnāṁ yata-cetasām
abhito brahma-nirvāṇaṁ
vartate viditātmanām

27. *sparśan kṛtvā bahir bāhyāṁś*
cakṣuś caivāntare bhruvoḥ
prāṇāpānau samau kṛtvā
nāsābhyantara-cāriṇau

28. *yatendriya-mano-buddhir*
munir mokṣa-parāyaṇaḥ
vigatecchā-bhaya-krodho
yaḥ sadā mukta eva saḥ

29. *bhoktāraṁ yajña-tapasāṁ*
sarva-loka-maheśvaram
suhṛdaṁ sarva-bhūtānāṁ
jñātvā māṁ śāntim ṛcchati

24. That person, happy within, who rejoices within, whose soul is enlightened, is an ascetic, is absorbed in God and has attained God.

25. Ascetics, who have gone beyond duality, whose moral imperfections have been washed away, who are self-restrained, delighting in the welfare of all beings, gain absorption in God.

26. Ascetics who control their minds, who liberate themselves from desire and anger, and who recognise God, dwell absorbed in God here and hereafter.

27-28. The sage, who withdraws from external contacts, who fixes his gaze between the eyebrows, who balances his incoming and outgoing breath, who controls the senses, mental powers and intellect, whose objective is liberation, who is free from desire, fear and anger, is certainly set free.

29. A person who knows Me to be the beneficiary of all spiritual sacrifice and religious austerities, Lord of the whole world and friend of all beings, attains peace.

Chapter Six

Deep, Abstract *Yoga* Meditation

Asceticism, the practice of *yoga* for self-purification, leads to freedom from desire, immunity from sorrow, bliss and union with God. One who falls from *yoga* practice takes birth again to continue in the next life. Of all *yogis* the most dear is the devotee.

Śrī Bhagavān uvāca

1 *anāśritaḥ karma-phalaṁ*
kāryaṁ karma karoti yaḥ
sa samnyāsī ca yogī ca
na niragnir na cākriyaḥ

2. *yaṁ samnyāsam iti prāhur*
yogaṁ taṁ viddhi pāṇḍava
na hy asamnyasta-saṅkalpo
yogī bhavati kaścana

3. *ārurukṣor muner yogaṁ*
karma kāraṇam ucyate
yogārūḍhasya tasyaiva
śamaḥ kāraṇam ucyate

4. *yadā hi nendriyārtheṣu*
na karmasv anuṣajjate
sarva-saṅkalpa-sannyāsī
yogārūḍhas tadocyate

5. *uddhared ātmanātmānaṁ*
nātmānam avasādayet
ātmaiva hy ātmano bandhur
ātmaiva ripur ātmanaḥ

6. *bandhur ātmātmanas tasya*
yenātmaivātmanā jitaḥ
anātmanas tu śatrutve
vartetātmaiva śatru-vat

7. *jitātmanaḥ praśāntasya*
paramātmā samāhitaḥ
śītoṣṇa-sukha-duḥkheṣu
tathā mānāpamānayoḥ

8. *jñāna-vijñāna-tṛptātmā*
kūṭa-stho vijitendriyaḥ
yukta ity ucyate yogī
sama-loṣṭāśma-kāñcanaḥ

The Lord said:

1. One who performs his duty unattached to its fruit, is an ascetic, a *yogi,* but not one, who does not light sacrificial fire and neglects his duty.

2. Renunciation is called *yoga,* son of Pandu, for no-one ever becomes a *yogi* or an ascetic without renouncing desire.

3. For a sage to attain *yoga,* religious activity is the way. When one has attained *yoga,* freedom from all the illusions of existence becomes the way.

4. When a person has renounced all desires, only then he attains *yoga,* being neither attached to sense-objects nor to fruitive activities.

5. One must elevate oneself by the mind. One must never lower oneself, for the mind can be either one's friend or enemy.

6. The mind, when conquered by the self, is a friend to the self, but when unconquered, the mind acts as an enemy to the self.

7. The self-controlled person has undisturbed inner peace and remains established in the Supreme Spirit, whether in heat or cold, pain or pleasure, honour or dishonour.

8. The ascetic who has subdued passion is unshakable, and being absorbed in meditation is fully contented with sacred knowledge, seeing a lump of earth, stones or gold as all the same.

9. *suhṛn-mitrāry-udāsīna*
madhyastha-dveṣya-bandhuṣu
sādhuṣv api ca pāpeṣu
sama-buddhir viśiṣyate

10. *yogī yuñjīta satatam*
ātmānaṁ rahasi sthitaḥ
ekākī yatac-ittātmā
nirāśīr aparigrahaḥ

11. *śucau deśe pratiṣṭhāpya*
sthiram āsanam ātmanaḥ
nāty-ucchritaṁ nāti-nīcam
cailājina-kuśottaram

12. *tatraikāgraṁ manaḥ kṛtvā*
yata-cittendriya-kriyaḥ
upaviśyāsane yuñjyād
yogam ātma-viśuddhaye

13. *samaṁ kāya-śiro-grīvaṁ*
dhārayann acalaṁ sthiraḥ
samprekṣya nāsikāgraṁ svaṁ
diśaś cānavalokayan

14. *praśāntātmā vigata-bhīr*
brahmacāri-vrate sthitaḥ
manaḥ saṁyamya mac-citto
yukta āsīta mat-paraḥ

15. *yuñjann evaṁ sadātmānaṁ*
yogī niyata-mānasaḥ
śāntiṁ nirvāṇa-paramāṁ
mat-saṁstham adhigacchati

16. *nāty-aśnatas tu yogo'sti*
na caikāntam anaśnataḥ
na cāti-svapna-śīlasya
jāgrato naiva cārjuna

9. Still better is one who bears an equal mind towards friends, enemies, relatives, strangers, mediators, the envious, the vicious or the virtuous.

10. An ascetic should always meditate in a secluded place controlling spirit and soul alone. One should be free from desire and feelings of possessiveness.

11. One should make a firm seat in a clean place covered with sacred grass, deerskin and a cloth, neither too high nor too low.

12. There the *yogi* should sit fixing the mind on one point only. One should conquer the fire of one's thoughts and senses and practise yoga for self-purification.

13-14. One should hold the body, head and neck upright. Motionless and steadfast, gaze upon the point of the nose without looking around. Peaceful, fearless, situated in the vow of celibacy and controlling the mind, one should meditate on Me. The yogi should be devoted to Me as the ultimate goal.

15. The yogi of subdued mind, constantly absorbed in meditation in such a manner, is in union with Me, and attains peace and supreme bliss.

16. One who eats to excess or one who starves oneself, cannot practise *yoga,* Arjuna, nor one who sleeps too much or does not sleep at all.

17. *yuktāhāra-vihārasya*
yukta-ceṣṭasya karmasu
yukta-svapnāvabodhasya
yogo bhavati duḥkha-hā

18. *yadā viniyataṁ cittam*
ātmany evāvatiṣṭhate
niḥspṛhaḥ sarva-kāmebhyo
yukta ity ucyate tadā

19. *yathā dīpo nivāta-stho*
neṅgate sopamā smṛtā
yogino yata-cittasya
yuñjato yogam ātmanaḥ

20. *yatroparamate cittaṁ*
niruddhaṁ yoga-sevayā
yatra caivātmanātmānaṁ
paśyann ātmani tuṣyati

21. *sukham ātyantikaṁ yat tad*
buddhi-grāhyam atīndriyam
vetti yatra na caivāyaṁ
sthitaś calati tattvataḥ

22. *yam labdhvā cāparaṁ lābhaṁ*
manyate nādhikaṁ tataḥ
yasmin sthito na duḥkhena
guruṇāpi vicālyate

23. *taṁ vidyād duḥkha-saṁyoga-*
viyogaṁ yoga-sañjñitam
sa niścayena yoktavyo
yogo' nirviṇṇa-cetasā

24. *saṅkalpa-prabhavān kāmāṁs*
tyaktvā sarvān aśeṣataḥ
manasaivendriya-grāmaṁ
viniyamya samantataḥ

17. *Yoga* alleviates pain from one who has control over eating, sleeping, wakefulness, relaxation and work.

18. When one, with a controlled mind, becomes situated in the Self alone, free from all kinds of desires, then, one is said to be established in *yoga.*

19. The *yogi* of controlled mind meditates unwaveringly on the Self, like a lamp that burns without a flicker in a place sheltered from the wind.

20. When one's mind, restrained by the practice of *yoga* becomes quiet, and when one rightly understands the Self, then, one is certainly satisfied in the Self.

21. One feels an endless bliss that is beyond the senses and is accessible through transcendental intelligence. Becoming established in it one does not depart from its truth.

22. And having found it, one believes no gain is greater. Established in it, one is not disturbed even by the deepest sorrow.

23. To be immune from sorrow, is known as *yoga.* This *yoga,* must be practised with an inspired mind and determination.

24. Entirely abandoning all desires arising from sentimental persuasion one restrains the mind from the senses completely.

25\. *śanaiḥ śanair uparamed*
buddhyā dhṛti-gṛhītayā
ātma-saṁsthaṁ manaḥ kṛtva
na kiñcid api cintayet

26\. *yato yato niścarati*
manaś cañcalam asthiram
tatas tato niyamyaitad
ātmany eva vaśam nayet

27\. *praśānta-manasaṁ hy enaṁ*
yoginaṁ sukham uttamam
upaiti śānta-rajasaṁ
brahma-bhūtam akalmaṣam

28\. *yuñjann evaṁ sadātmānaṁ*
yogī vigata-kalmaṣah
sukhena brahma-saṁsparśam
atyantaṁ sukham aśnute

29\. *sarva-bhūta-stham ātmānaṁ*
sarva-bhūtānī cātmani
īkṣate yoga-yuktātmā
sarvatra sama-darśanaḥ

30\. *yo māṁ paśyati sarvatra*
sarvaṁ ca mayi paśyati
tasyāham na praṇaśyāmi
sa ca me na praṇaśyati

31\. *sarva-bhūta-sthitaṁ yo māṁ*
bhajaty ekatvam āsthitaḥ
sarvathā vartamāno' pi
sa yogī mayi vartate

32\. *ātmaupamyena sarvatra*
samaṁ paśyati yo' rjuna
sukham vā yadi vā duḥkhaṁ
sa yogī paramo mataḥ

25. Armed with constancy and resolution and by means of the intellect, one gradually attains peace. With the mind fixed on the Self, one thinks of nothing else.

26. Whenever the confused, uncertain mind wanders away, subdue it and bring it back under the control of the self.

27. The *yogi* whose mind is composed, passionless, and pure, who is absorbed in God, attains the highest bliss.

28. The yogi, always concentrating the mind on the self, free from sin, comes into close contact with God and enjoys endless bliss.

29. Absorbed in *yoga*, seeing the spark of God within all beings, and all beings within God, one sees God in everything.

30. One who sees Me everywhere, and sees everything in Me, never loses Me, nor is ever lost to Me.

31. One who is united with Me, who worships Me, Who am in all beings, that yogi, whatever the circumtances may be, always lives in Me.

32. That yogi, who, by analogy to his own self, sees everyone equally both in pleasure and pain, is considered the most excellent, Arjuna.

Arjuna uvāca

33. *yo'yaṁ yogas tvayā proktaḥ*
sāmyena mashusūdana
etasyāham na paśyāmi
cañcalatvāt sthitiṁ sthirām

34. *cañcalaṁ hi manaḥ kṛṣṇa*
pramāthi balavad dṛḍham
tasyāhaṁ nigraham manye
vāyor iva su-duṣkaram

Śrī Bhagavān uvāca

35. *asaṁśayaṁ mahā-bāho*
mano durnigrahaṁ calam
abhyāsena tu kaunteya
vairāgyeṇa ca gṛhyate

36. *asaṁyātatmanā yogo*
duṣprāpa iti me matiḥ
vaśyātmanā tu yatatā
śakyo' vāptum upāyataḥ

Arjuna uvāca

37. *ayatiḥ śraddhayopeto*
yogāc calita-mānasaḥ
aprāpya yoga-saṁsiddhim
kāṁ gatiṁ kṛṣṇa gacchati

38. *kaccin nobhaya-vibhraṣṭaś*
chinnābhram iva naśyati
apratiṣṭho mahā-bāho
vimūḍho brahmaṇaḥ pathi

39. *etan me saṁśayam kṛṣṇa*
chettum arhasy aśeṣataḥ
tvad-anyaḥ saṁśayasyāsya
chettā na hy upapadyate

Arjuna said:

33. O Madhusudana, I cannot see how this *yoga* of equanimity which You have taught, can be firmly established for the restless mind.

34. The mind is deviant, tormenting, wilful and strong, O Krishna. I think it is very difficult to restrain, like trying to restrain the wind.

The Lord said:

35. The mind, without doubt, is difficult to restrain, O mighty-armed son of Kunti, but it is possible by practice and asceticism to restrain it.

36. In My opinion, one cannot attain *yoga* with an unbridled-mind, but if one strives by appropriate means to control the mind one can attain *yoga*.

Arjuna said:

37. What is the outcome for a person who has faith, yet cannot restrain the mind, thus deviating from *yoga* and not attaining perfection, O Krishna?

38. For one who is perplexed and fluctuates on the path of *yoga*, are they not like a patch of separated cloud that evaporates, losing both spiritual and material success?

39. Please Krishna, allow me to ask You to clarify my doubt completely, for there is no-one but You who can remove this doubt.

Śrī Bhagavān uvāca

40. *pārtha naiveha nāmutra*
vināśas tasya vidyate
na hi kalyāṇa-kṛt kaścid
durgatiṁ tāta gacchati

41. *prāpya puṇya-kṛtāṁ lokān*
uṣitvā śāśvatīh samāḥ
śucīnāṁ śrīmatāṁ gehe
yoga-bhraṣṭo' bhijāyate

42. *atha vā yoginām eva*
kule bhavati dhīmatām
etad dhi durlabhataraṁ
loke janma yad īdṛśam

43. *tatra taṁ buddhi-saṁyogaṁ*
labhate paurva-dehikam
yatate ca tato bhūyaḥ
saṁsiddhau kuru-nandana

44. *pūrvābhyāsena tenaiva*
hriyate hy avaśo' pi saḥ
jijñāsur api yogasya
śabda-brahmātivartate

45. *prayatnād yatamānas tu*
yogī saṁśuddha-kilbiṣaḥ
aneka-janma-saṁsiddhas
tato yāti parāṁ gatim

46. *tapasvibhyo' dhiko yogī*
jñānibhyo' pi mato' dhikaḥ
karmibhyaś cādhiko yogī
tasmād yogī bhavārjuna

47. *yoginām api sarveṣāṁ*
mad-gatenāntar-ātmanā
śraddhāvan bhajate yo māṁ
sa me yuktatamo mataḥ

The Lord said:

40. No destruction comes to such a person, Partha, neither here nor in the next world. One who does good is not vanquished by distress, My friend.

41. Such a person lives for innumerable years in the worlds of the virtuous. But one who falls from the practice of *yoga* is reborn in the home of a pious and auspicious family.

42. Or one is born in the family of wise ascetics. Such a birth is indeed rare in this world.

43. There one regains the knowledge derived from former existences and strives still further for complete success, O descendent of Kuru.

44. One's previous practice leads one on, almost automatically. And also, one who wishes to understand *yoga* goes beyond the conventions of scriptures.

45. Purified from sins, perfected through many births, the *yogi* perseveres with active efforts and reaches the final beatitude.

46. The *yogi* is regarded as superior to ascetics, superior to wise men and superior to ritualists. Therefore be a *yogi,* Arjuna.

47. And of all *yogis,* one who abides in Me with all one's heart, who meditates on Me, who worships Me with faith, I regard as the most devoted.

CHAPTER SEVEN

The *Yoga* of Sacred Knowledge

Knowledge of how the Lord is present in every element of nature, the universe, the sacred mantras, our qualities and attitudes is described. There are four kinds of people recognised by Krishna who find liberation in this way, whereas the ignorant become more entangled in material nature.

Śrī Bhagavān uvāca

1. *mayy āsakta-manāḥ pārtha*
yogaṁ yuñjan mad-āśrayaḥ
asaṁśayaṁ samagraṁ māṁ
yathā jñāsyasi tac chṛṇu

2. *jñānaṁ te' haṁ sa-vijñānam*
idaṁ vakṣyāmy aśeṣataḥ
yaj jñātvā neha bhūyo' nyaj
jñātavyam avaśiṣyate

3. *manuṣyāṇāṁ sahasreṣu*
kaścid yatati siddhaye
yatatām api siddhānāṁ
kaścin māṁ vetti tattvataḥ

4. *bhūmir āpo' nalo vāyuḥ*
khaṁ mano buddhir eva ca
ahaṁkāra itīyaṁ me
bhinnā prakṛtir aṣṭadhā

5. *apareyāṁ itas tv anyam*
prakṛtiṁ viddhi me parām
jīva-bhūtāṁ mahā-bāho
yayedaṁ dhāryate jagat

6. *etad-yonīnī bhūtāni*
sarvāṇīty upadhāraya
ahaṁ kṛtsnasya jagataḥ
prabhavaḥ pralayas tathā

7. *mattaḥ parataraṁ nānyat*
kiñcid asti dhanañjaya
mayi sarvam idaṁ protaṁ
sūtre maṇi-gaṇā iva

8. *raso' ham apsu kaunteya*
prabhāsmi śaśi-sūryayoḥ
praṇavaḥ sarva-vedeṣu
śabdaḥ khe pauruṣaṁ nṛṣu

The Lord said:

1. Hear from Me Partha, how you will fully know Me without doubt when you practise *yoga* with your mind attached to Me, seeking shelter in Me.

2. I shall teach you such knowledge endowed with the right understanding, knowing which, nothing else shall remain to be known in this world.

3. Among thousands of people, one may persevere for perfection; yet even among those perfected, hardly one may know Me in truth.

4. My material world is eight-fold. It is divided into earth, water, fire, air, ether, mind, intellect and also self-consciousness.

5. Know, mighty warrior, that the material world is inferior. There is a higher world which is the very life that upholds this material world.

6. Know, these two worlds are the source of all beings. I am the origin and I am the end of the entire universe.

7. There is nothing higher than Me, O conqueror of wealth. Everything is strung on Me like pearls on a thread.

8. I am the flavour in water, O son of Kunti, the splendour in the moon and the sun. I am the sacred syllable Om in all the Vedas, the primeval sound in ether and the masculine strength in men.

9. *puṇyo gandhaḥ pṛthivyāṁ ca*
tejaś cāsmi vibhāvasau
jīvanaṁ sarva-bhūteṣu
tapaś cāsmi tapasviṣu

10. *bījaṁ māṁ sarva-bhūtānāṁ*
viddhi pārtha sanātanam
buddhir buddhimatām asmi
tejas tejasvinām aham

11. *balaṁ balavatāṁ cāhaṁ*
kāma-rāga-vivarjitam
dharmāviruddho bhūteṣu
kāmo' smi bharatarṣabha

12. *ye caiva sāttvikā bhāvā*
rājasās tāmasāś ca ye
matta eveti tān viddhi
na tv ahaṁ teṣu te mayi

13. *tribhir guṇa-mayair bhāvair*
ebhiḥ sarvam idaṁ jagat
mohitaṁ nābhijānāti
mām ebhyaḥ param avyayam

14. *daivī hy eṣā guṇa-mayī*
māmā mayā duratyayā
mām eva ye āprapadyante
māyam etāṁ taranti te

15. *na māṁ duṣkṛtino mūḍhāḥ*
prapadyante narādhamāḥ
māyayāpahṛta-jñānā
āsuram bhāvam āśritāḥ

16. *catur-vidhā bhajante māṁ*
janāḥ sukṛtino' rjuna
ārto jijñāsur arthārthī
jñānī ca bharatarṣabha

9. I am the sweet-scented fragrance of earth, the brilliance of fire, the life in all beings, and the asceticism in ascetics.

10. Son of Partha, know Me as the everlasting seed in all living beings, the intelligence of the intelligent, and the splendour of the splendid.

11. I am the strength of the strong, free from desire and lust. And in living beings, O best of the Bharatas, I am desire consistent with virtue.

12. Whatever mental attitudes arise from goodness, passion or ignorance, know them to come verily from Me; yet I am not in them; they are in Me.

13. These three principles of material nature, goodness, passion and ignorance, delude this world which does not know that I am imperishable and the most high.

14. This divine illusion of Mine, based on the three *gunas,* is very hard to overcome. But those who take refuge in Me, can overcome this illusion.

15. Evil-doers, the degraded, and the indolent do not take refuge in Me. Their Illusion deprives them of knowledge and they attach themselves to the infernal nature.

16. Four kinds of virtuous people worship Me, Arjuna. Those who are struck by calamity, those who seek knowledge, those who seek wealth and those who are wise, O prince.

17. *teṣāṁ jñānī nitya-yukta*
eka-bhaktir viśiṣyate
priyo hi jñānino' tyartham
ahaṁ sa ca mama priyaḥ

18. *udārāḥ sarva evaite*
jñānī tv ātmaiva me matam
āsthitaḥ sa hi yuktātmā
mām evānuttamāṁ gatim

19. *bahūnāṁ janmanām ante*
jñānavān māṁ prapadyate
vāsudevaḥ sarvam iti
sa mahātmā su-durlabhaḥ

20. *kāmais tais tair hṛta-jñānāḥ*
prapadyante' nya-devatāḥ
taṁ taṁ niyamam āsthāya
prakṛtyā niyatāḥ svayā

21. *yo yo yāṁ yāṁ tanuṁ bhaktaḥ*
śraddhayārcitum icchati
tasya tasyācalāṁ śradhāṁ
tām eva vidadhāmy aham

22. *sa tayā śraddhayā yuktas*
tasyārādhanam īhate
labhate ca tataḥ kāmān
mayaiva vihitān hi tān

23. *antavat tu phalaṁ teṣāṁ*
tad bhavaty alpa-medhasām
devān deva-yājo yanti
mad-bhaktā yānti mām api

24. *avyaktaṁ vyaktim āpannaṁ*
manyante mām abuddhayaḥ
paraṁ bhāvam ajānanto
mamāvyayam anuttamam

17. Always devoted and intent upon Me alone, the wise person is best amongst them. Certainly, I am very dear to him and he is dear to Me.

18. All these great souls are certainly noble, but one who is wise is just like myself, for he is highly devoted and becomes established in Me, the highest goal.

19. After many births, a wise person takes refuge in Me, realising that I, Lord Krishna, am all there is. Such a great soul is very rare.

20. Those, deprived of knowledge by so many desires, seek other gods. Led by their own nature, they follow various rituals.

21. For any devotee who wishes to worship Me with faith, in whatever form, I make that faith steady.

22. Endowed with that faith, the devotee exerts himself in the worship of his chosen deity and obtains his desires. But in truth it is I who grant these desires.

23. But the fruits these people of little understanding obtain are really limited. Worshippers of other gods go to them. My devotees come to Me.

24. Ignorant people think that first I was unmanifest and then became manifest. They do not know My higher nature which is imperishable and incomparable.

25. *nāhaṁ prakāśaḥ sarvasya*
yoga-māyā-samāvṛtaḥ
mūḍho' yaṁ nābhijānāti
loko mām ajam avyayam

26. *vedāhaṁ samatītāni*
vartamānāni cārjuna
bhaviṣyāṇi ca bhūtāni
māṁ tu veda na kaścana

27. *icchā-dveṣa-samutthena*
dvandva-mohena bhārata
sarva-bhūtāni saṁmohaṁ
sarge yānti paraṁtapa

28. *yeṣāṁ tv anta-gataṁ pāpaṁ*
janānāṁ puṇya-karmaṇām
te dvandva-moha-nirmuktā
bhajante māṁ dṛḍha-vratāḥ

29. *jarā-marana-mokṣāya*
mām āśritya yatanti ye
te brahma tad viduḥ kṛtsnam
adhyātmaṁ karma cākhilam

30. *sādhibhutādhidaivaṁ māṁ*
sādhiyajñaṁ ca ye viduḥ
prayāṇa-kāle' pi ca māṁ
te vidur yukta-cetasaḥ

25. I am not visible to everyone. I am concealed behind the veil of illusion. This bewildered world knows not that I am unborn and imperishable.

26. I know the past, present and future of all beings, but no one knows Me, Arjuna.

27. All beings enter illusion at birth, O destroyer of the enemies. They are bewildered by the dualities that arise from desire and hate, Bharata.

28. When the deeds of the virtuous bring their sins to an end, they are liberated from the illusion of duality, and thus they serve Me with determination.

29. Those who seek refuge in Me, and strive for liberation from decay and death, fully understand *brahman,* the individual self, and all religious activities.

30. Those who are conscious of Me, who know Me as the spiritual substratum of the material world, the foundation of the demigods, the presiding deity of all sacrifice, truly know Me even at the time of death.

Chapter Eight

Attaining the Imperishable

By being fully absorbed in meditating on the Supreme Spirit in life one transcends the constantly remanifesting world and attains the perfected state at death, beyond the cycle of birth and death.

Arjuna uvāca

1. *kiṁ tad brahma kim adhyātmaṁ*
kiṁ karma puruṣottama
adhibhūtaṁ ca kim proktam
adhidaivaṁ kim ucyate

2. *adhiyajñaḥ kathaṁ ko' tra*
dehe' smin madhusūdana
prayāṇa-kāle ca kathaṁ
jñeyo' si niyatatāmabhiḥ

Śrī Bhagavān uvāca

3. *akṣaraṁ brahma paramaṁ*
svabhāvo' dhyātmam ucyate
bhūta-bhāvodbhava-karo
visargaḥ karma-sañjñitaḥ

4. *adhibhūtaṁ kṣaro bhāvaḥ*
puruṣaś cādḥidaivatam
adhiyajño' ham evātra
dehe dehabhṛtāṁ vara

5. *anta-kāle ca mām eva*
smaran muktvā kalevaram
yaḥ prayāti sa mad-bhāvam
yāti nāsty atra saṁśayaḥ

6. *yaṁ yaṁ vāpī smaran bhāvaṁ*
tyajaty ante kalevaram
taṁ tam evaiti kaunteya
sadā tad-bhāva-bhāvitaḥ

7. *tasmāt sarveṣu kāleṣu*
mām anusmara yudhya ca
mayy arpita-mano-buddhir
mām evaiṣyasy asaṁśayam

Arjuna said:

1. O Supreme Person what is *brahman*? What is the self? What is *karma*? What is material existence and what are the demigods?

2. Who is the Lord of sacrifice in this body, O Madhusudana? And how can You be known by men of self-control at the time of death?

The Lord said:

3. *Brahman* is imperishable and supreme. His eternal nature is called *adhiyatma,* the self. Action which determines the state of existence of a being, is called *karma.*

4. Material existence is that manifestation which is perishable by nature, O prince. The *purusha,* soul of the universe is a manifestation of the Supreme Himself and includes all the demigods. Indeed, I Myself am here in the heart of everybody as the lord of sacrifice.

5. And whoever leaves his body, thinking of Me at the time of death, attains My nature. Of this there is no doubt.

6. When a person eventually leaves this body he will enter whatever state of being his mind has always been absorbed in, Kaunteya.

7. Therefore, always think of Me, and fight. If you fix your mind and intelligence on Me, without doubt, you will come to Me.

8. *abhyāsa-yoga-yuktena*
cetasā nānya-gāminā
paramaṁ puruṣaṁ divyaṁ
yāti pārthānucintayan

9. *kaviṁ purāṇam anuśāsitāram*
aṇor aṇīyāṁsam anusmared yaḥ
sarvasya dhātāram acintya-rūpam
āditya-varṇaṁ tamasaḥ parastāt

10. *prayāṇa-kāle manasācalena*
bhaktyā yukto yoga-balena caiva
bhruvor madhye prāṇam āveśya samyak
sa taṁ paraṁ puruṣam upaiti divyam

11. *yad akṣaraṁ veda-vido vadanti*
viśanti yad yatayo vīta-rāgāḥ
yad icchanto brahmacaryaṁ caranti
tat te padaṁ saṅgraheṇa pravakṣye

12. *sarva-dvārāṇi saṁyamya*
mano hṛdi nirudhya ca
mūrdhny ādhāyātmanaḥ prāṇam
āsthito yoga-dhāraṇām

13. *om ity ekākṣaraṁ brahma*
vyāharan mam ānusmaran
yaḥ prayāti tyajan dehaṁ
sa yāti paramāṁ gatim

14. *ananya-cetāḥ satataṁ*
yo māṁ smarati nityaśaḥ
tasyāhaṁ sulabhaḥ pārtha
nitya-yuktasya yoginaḥ

8. One who constantly meditates on the Supreme Divine Being with an undeviated and disciplined mind, is sure to reach Him, Partha.

9. One should meditate on God as
   The ruler
   Timeless in origin
   Knower of past, present and future
   Smaller than an atom of matter
   Beyond darkness
   Bestower of everything
   Luminous like the sun
   With inconceivable form.

10. The person who meditates on God at the time of death with undeviating mind, in full devotion, and who by strength of *yoga*, wholly concentrates his life-breath between the eyebrows, reaches that Supreme Being.

11. Knowers of the Vedas call it the imperishable sacred syllable Om. Ascetics freed from passion enter into it. Those who desire it, lead a life of continence and chastity. I will explain it to you briefly.

12. One should control all the openings of the body, confine one's mind within the heart, concentrate one's life-breath in the head and dwell in *yoga*.

13. The person who utters the sacred syllable Om, who remembers Me when leaving the body, attains the highest goal.

14. I am easily attained by the ascetic, who constantly gives his undivided thoughts to Me, who always remembers Me and who is intent on Me, Partha.

15. *ṃām upetya punar janma*
duḥkhālayam aśāśvatam
nāpnuvanti mahātmānaḥ
saṁsiddhiṁ paramāṁ gatāḥ

16. *ā-brahma-bhuvanāl lokāḥ*
punar āvartino' rjuna
mām upetya tu kaunteya
punar janma na vidyate

17. *sahasra-yuga-paryantam*
ahar yad brahmaṇo viduḥ
rātriṁ yuga-sahasrāntāṁ
te' ho-rātra-vido janāḥ

18. *avyaktād vyakatayaḥ sarvāḥ*
prabhavanty ahar-āgame
rātry-āgame pralīyante
tatraivāvyakta-sañjñake

19. *bhūta-grāmaḥ sa evāyaṁ*
bhūtvā bhūtvā pralīyate
rātry-āgame' vaśaḥ pārtha
prabhavaty ahar-āgame

20. *paras tasmāt tu bhāvo' nyo'*
vyakto' vyaktāt sanātanaḥ
yaḥ sa sarveṣu bhūteṣu
naśyatsu na vinaśyati

21. *avyakto' kṣara ity uktas*
tam āhuḥ paramāṁ gatim
yaṁ prāpya na nivartante
tad dhāma paramaṁ mama

22. *puruṣaḥ sa paraḥ pārtha*
bhaktyā labhyas tv ananyayā
yasyāntaḥ-sthāni bhūtāni
yena sarvam idaṁ tatam

CHAPTER NINE

The Highest Mystical Knowledge

Krishna is the imperishable originator of all beings. He is everything, the beneficiary of all sacrifices and the goal of all worship. By worshipping Him with love one will attain Him.

Śrī Bhagavān uvāca

1. *idaṁ tu te guhyatamaṁ*
pravakṣyāmy anasūyave
jñānaṁ vijñāna-sahitaṁ
yaj jñātvā mokṣyase' śubhāt

2. *rāja-vidyā rāja-guhyaṁ*
pavitṛam idam uttamam
pratyakṣāvagamaṁ dharmyaṁ
su-sukhaṁ kartum avyayam

3. *aśraddadhānāḥ puruṣā*
dharmasyāsya parantapa
aprāpya māṁ nivartante
mṛtyu-saṁsāra-vartmani

4. *mayā tatam idaṁ sarvaṁ*
jagad avyakta-mūrtinā
mat-sthāni sarva-bhūtāni
na cāhaṁ teṣv avasthitaḥ

5. *na ca mat-sthāni bhūtāni*
paśya me yogam aiśvaram
bhūta-bhṛn na ca bhūta-stho
mamātmā bhuta-bhāvanaḥ

6. *yathākāśa-sthito nityaṁ*
vāyuḥ sarvatra-go mahān
tathā sarvāṇi bhūtāni
mat-sthānīty upadhāraya

7. *sarva-bhūtāni kaunteya*
prakṛtim yānti māmikām
kalpa-kṣaye punas tāni
kalpādau visṛjamy aham

The Lord said:

1. Because you are not an envious person, I shall therefore impart to you the highest mystical knowledge and realization, knowing which you will be liberated from sin.

2. It is the crown of science
   The greatest mystery
   The best purifier
   Plainly understandable
   Endowed with virtuous qualities
   Easy to practise
   And imperishable.

3. Those who have no faith in these spiritual practices, do not reach Me, O mighty warrior. They return to the endless cycle of births and deaths.

4. The whole universe is pervaded by Me in My imperceptible form. All beings abide in Me, but I do not abide in them.

5. Behold My mystic prowess. All beings abide in Me, I sustain all beings, yet I am not in them. Although I am beyond all manifestation, I Myself am the source of everything.

6. Try to understand, all beings abide in Me just like the strong wind is omnipresent in the sky.

7. At the end of a *kalpa* (a period of 4,320 million years, all beings enter into My nature, *prakriti.* And at the beginning of another *kalpa,* I send them forth again, Kaunteya.

8. *prakṛtiṁ svām avaṣṭabhya*
visṛjāmi punah punaḥ
bhūta-grāmam imaṁ kṛtsnam
avaśaṁ prakṛter vaśāt

9. *na ca māṁ tāni karmāṇi*
nibadhnanti dhanañjaya
udāsīnad āsīnam
asaktaṁ teṣu karmasu

10. *mayādhyakṣeṇa prakṛtiḥ*
sūyate sa-carācaram
hetunānena kaunteya
jagad viparivartate

11. *avajāṇanti māṁ mūḍha*
mānuṣīṁ tanum āśritam
paraṁ bhāvam ajānanto
mama bhūta-maheśvaram

12. *moghāśā mogha-karmāṇo*
mogha-jñānā vicetasaḥ
rākṣasīṁ āsurīṁ caiva
prakṛtiṁ mohinīṁ śritāḥ

13. *mahātmānas tu māṁ pārtha*
daivīṁ prakṛtim āśritāḥ
bhajanty ananya-manaso
jñātvā bhūtādim avyayam

14. *satataṁ kīrtayanto māṁ*
yatantaś ca dṛḍha-vratāḥ
namasyantaś ca māṁ bhaktyā
nitya-yuktā upāsate

15. *jñāna-yajñena cāpy anye*
yajanto mām upāsate
ekatvena pṛthaktvena
bahudhā viśvato-mukham

8. This multitude of beings is absorbed into My nature. I oblige them to go forth again and again by virtue of that nature.

9. These activities do not bind Me, Arjuna. I remain neutral and unattached.

10. Under My supervision nature produces all animate and inanimate beings. This is what causes the world to revolve, Kaunteya.

11. Fools do not acknowledge Me when I take a human form, for they do not know My transcendental nature as the Lord of all beings.

12. These atheists are perplexed, deluded and demoniac. Their hopes, actions and knowledge are vain and they cling to their infernal nature.

13. But great souls take shelter of My divine nature, Partha.They know Me as the imperishable originator of all beings and they serve Me with undivided attention.

14. Always striving to glorify Me and paying obeisances to Me, steady in discipline and with firm vows, they continually worship Me with devotion.

15. And others, who make sacrifices to acquire knowledge, worship Me in many ways. I am the One whose face is turned to every direction.

16. *ahaṁ kratur ahaṁ yajñaḥ*
svadhāham aham auṣadham
mantro' ham aham evājyam
aham agnir ahaṁ hutam

17. *pitāham asya jagato*
mātā dhātā pitāmahaḥ
vedyaṁ pavitram ouṅkāra
ṛk sāma yajur eva ca

18. *gatir bhartā prabhuḥ śakṣī*
nivāsaḥ śaraṇaṁ suhṛt
prabhavaḥ pralayaḥ sthānaṁ
nidhānaṁ bījam avyayam

19. *tapāmy aham ahaṁ varṣaṁ*
nigṛhṇāmy utsṛjāmi ca
amṛtaṁ caiva mṛtyuś ca
sad asac cāham arjuna

20. *trai-vidyā māṁ soma-pāḥ pūta-pāpā*
yajñair iṣṭvā svargatiṁ prārthayante
te puṇyam āsādya surrendra-lokam
aśnanti divyān divi deva-bhogān

21. *te taṁ bhuktvā svarga-lokaṁ viśālaṁ*
kṣīṇe puṇye martya-lokaṁ viśanti
evaṁ trayī-dharmam anuprapannā
gatāgataṁ kāma-kāmā labhante

22. *ananyāś cintayanto māṁ*
ye janāḥ paryupāsate
teṣāṁ nityābhiyuktānāṁ
yoga-kṣemaṁ vahāmy aham

23. *ye'py anya-devatā-bhaktā*
yajante śraddhayānvitāḥ
te'pi mam eva kaunteya
yajanty avidhi-pūrvakam

16. I am the sacrificial rite, I am the sacrifice
I am the offering for the ancestors
And I am the healing herbs
I am the sacred mantra addressed to any individual deity
I am the clarified butter to anoint any offering
And I am the fire.

17. I am the father, mother, support and grandfather of the universe. I am what is to be known. I am the purifier, the sacred and mystical syllable *Om.* I am also the *Rig, Sama* and *Yajur Vedas.*

18. I am the Lord, your goal, maintainer, witness, abode, refuge and good-hearted friend. I am the cause of existence, the dissolution, province of the demigods, place of rest and the imperishable seed.

19. I give heat
I send and withhold the rain
I am immortality and mortality
I am existence and non-existence also, Arjuna.

20. The knowers of the Vedas, purified of sins, drink *soma* juice and worship Me with sacrifices, praying to attain heaven. They reach the world of the Lord of the demigods and enjoy heavenly pleasures.

21. After they have enjoyed the vast celestial world, their religious merit exhausted, they return to the world of mortals, to earth. Thus they conform to the duties of the Vedas. But those who follow their passions, return to the world of birth and death.

22. But for those who meditate on Me, unhampered by any other thoughts, worshipping Me, always fixed in devotion, I provide for their welfare and protect them.

23. Even those devotees, endowed with faith, worshipping other gods, worship Me alone, but without proper understanding, Kaunteya.

24. *ahaṁ hi sarva-yajñānāṁ*
bhoktā ca prabhur eva ca
na tu mām abhijānanti
tattvenātaś cyavanti te

25. *yānti deva-vratā devān*
pitṝn yānti pitṛ-vratāḥ
bhūtāni yānti bhūtejyā
yānti mad-yājino' pi mām

26. *patraṁ puṣpaṁ phalaṁ toyaṁ*
yo me bhaktyā prayacchati
tad ahaṁ bhakty-upahṛtam
aśnāmi prayatātmanaḥ

27. *yat karoṣi yad aśnāsi*
yaj juhoṣi dadāsi yat
yat tapasyasi kaunteya
tat kuruṣva mad-arpaṇam

28. *śubhāśubha-phalair evaṁ*
mokṣyase karma-bandhanaiḥ
sannyāsa-yoga-yuktātmā
vimukto mam upaiṣyasi

29. *samo' haṁ sarva-bhūteṣu*
na me dveṣyo' sti na priyaḥ
ye bhajanti tu māṁ bhaktyā
mayi te teṣu cāpy aham

30. *api cet su-durācāro*
bhajate mām ananya-bhāk
sādhur eva sa mantavyaḥ
samyag vyavasito hi saḥ

31. *kṣipraṁ bhavati dharmātmā*
śaśvac-chāntiṁ nigacchati
kaunteya pratijānīhi
na me bhaktaḥ praṇaśyati

24. I am the sole beneficiary and Lord of all sacrifices. But those who do not recognise Me in reality, fall down.

25. Worshippers of the demigods go to the demigods. Worshippers of ancestral spirits go to the ancestors. Worshippers of demons go to the demons, and My worshippers come to Me.

26. Whoever offers Me a leaf, a flower, a fruit or water with love and pure mind, I accept that offering of love.

27. Whatever you do, whatever you eat, intend to sacrifice, give away, or whatever religious austerity you observe, do it as an offering to Me, Kaunteya.

28. Thus you will be released from the bonds of *karma* and its results, good or evil. With mind absorbed in the *yoga* of renunciation, you will be liberated and come to Me.

29. I am impartial towards all beings. No one is either more or less dear to Me. But those who serve Me with devotion, they are in Me and I in them.

30. Even a profligate who worships Me thinking of no-one but Me, must be considered wise, because his determination is rightly directed.

31. That person soon becomes religious and obtains everlasting peace. My devotee never perishes, I promise, O son of Kunti.

32. *maṁ hi pārtha vyapāśritya*
ye'pi syuḥ pāpa-yonayaḥ
striyo vaiśyās tathā śūdrās
te' pi yānti parāṁ gatim

33. *kiṁ punar brāḥmaṇāḥ puṇyā*
bhaktā rājarṣayas tathā
anityam asukhaṁ lokam
imaṁ prāpya bhajasva mām

34. *man-manā bhava mad-bhakto*
mad-yājī māṁ namaskuru
mām evaiṣyasi yuktvaivam
ātmānaṁ mat-parāyaṇaḥ

32. Certainly those who take shelter in My teachings, whatever their birth, gender or employment, attain the highest goal, Partha.

33. How much more this is so of the virtuous, the devotees, the saintly kings who have come into this uncertain, painful world and serve Me with love.

34. Think of Me
Sacrifice to Me
Bow down to Me
Be absorbed in Me
Thus devoted, you will come to Me.

CHAPTER TEN

The Omnipresent Lord

Krishna details how He can be recognised in every aspect of the universal manifestation, which He supports with just a fractional part of Himself. His glories are endless. He illuminates the minds of those who recognise this and are constantly devoted to Him.

Śrī Bhagavān uvāca

1. *bhūya eva mahābāho*
śṛṇu me paramaṁ vacaḥ
yat te' haṁ prīyamāṇāya
vakṣyāmi hita-kāmyayā

2. *na me viduḥ sura-gaṇāḥ*
prabhavaṁ na maharṣayaḥ
aham ādir hi devānāṁ
maharṣīṇāṁ ca sarvaśaḥ

3. *yo māṁ ajam anādiṁ ca*
vetti loka-maheśvaram
asammūḍhaḥ sa martyeṣu
sarva-pāpaiḥ pramucyate

4. *buddhir jñānam asammohaḥ*
kṣamā satyaṁ damaḥ śamaḥ
sukhaṁ duhkhaṁ bhavo' bhāvo
bhayaṁ cābhayam eva ca

5. *ahiṁsā samatā tuṣṭis*
ṭapo dānaṁ yaśo' yaśaḥ
bhavanti bhāvā bhūtānāṁ
matta eva pṛthag-vidhāḥ

6. *maharṣayaḥ sapta pūrve*
catvāro manavas tathā
mad-bhāva mānasā jātā
yeṣāṁ loka imāḥ prajāḥ

7. *etāṁ vibhūtiṁ yogaṁ ca*
mama yo vetti tattvataḥ
so'vikampena yogena
yujyate nātra saṁśayaḥ

8. *ahaṁ sarvasya prabhavo*
mattaḥ sarvaṁ pravartate
iti matvā bhajante māṁ
budhā bhāva-samanvitāḥ

The Lord said:

1. Listen to My supreme word again, mighty warrior. Out of love for you and for your benefit, I shall declare further knowledge for your pleasure.

2. Neither the hosts of demigods, nor great sages know My origin, for, in every respect, I am the beginning of the demigods and the great sages.

3. One who knows Me as unborn and eternal, the Supreme Lord of the worlds, is undeluded among mortals and freed from all sins.

4-5. Perception, knowledge, composure, forgiveness, truthfulness, self-control, control of the senses, joy, sorrow, birth, death, fear and fearlessness, harmlessness, equanimity, contentment, religious austerity, charity, honour and dishonour, all these different kinds of dispositions in living beings arise from Me alone.

6. The seven great sages of ancient times and the four progenitors of mankind are created by Me. From them all creatures are brought forth in this world.

7. One who knows this supreme dominion and mystic power of Mine, becomes absorbed in spiritual discipline without hesitation. There is no doubt of this.

8. I am the origin of all. From Me everything arises. The wise know this and adore Me with great attention.

9. *mac-cittā mad-gata-prāṇā*
bodhayantaḥ parasparam
kathayantaś ca māṁ nityaṁ
tuṣyanti ca ramanti ca

10. *teṣāṁ satata-yuktānāṁ*
bhajatāṁ prīti-pūrvakam
dadāmi buddhi-yogaṁ taṁ
yena mām upayānti te

11. *teṣām evānukampārtham*
aham ajñāna-jaṁ tamaḥ
nāśayāmy ātma-bhāva-stho
jñāna-dīpena bhāsvatā

Arjuna uvāca

12. *paraṁ brahma paraṁ dhāma*
pavitraṁ paramaṁ bhavān
puruṣaṁ śāśvataṁ divyam
ādi-devam ajaṁ vibhum

13. *āhus tvām ṛṣayaḥ sarve*
devarṣir nāradas tathā
asito devalo vyāsaḥ
svayaṁ caiva bravīṣi me

14. *sarvam etad ṛtaṁ manye*
yam māṁ vadasi keśava
na hi te bhagavan vyaktiṁ
vidur devā na dānavāḥ

15. *svayam evātmanātmānaṁ*
vettha tvaṁ puruṣottama
bhūta-bhāvana bhūteśa
deva-deva jagat-pate

16. *vaktum arhasy aśeṣeṇa*
divyā hy ātma-vibhūtayaḥ
yābhir vibhūtibhir lokān
imāṁs tvaṁ vyāpya tiṣṭhasi

9. Always thinking of Me, their lives dedicated to Me, enlightening one another, and conversing about Me, they are forever happy and contented.

10. To those who are constantly devoted, who serve Me with love, I endow them with the intellect to reach Me.

11. Out of compassion I remove the mental darkness, born of spiritual ignorance which dwells in them, with the glowing lamp of knowledge.

Arjuna said:

12-13. You are the supreme God, supreme spirit, soul of the universe, best purifying prayer, transcendental, unborn, omnipresent and the highest abode. All the great sages such as Narada, Asita, Devala and Vyasa have declared this. And now You are personally telling me so Yourself.

14. I accept all that You say to Me as true, O Krishna. Neither demigods nor demons can truly perceive Your individuality.

15. O Supreme Spirit
God of gods
Lord of the world
Creator, Lord of living beings
You are understood by You alone.

16. Your manifestations are divine. Indeed they pervade all these worlds. Please, Lord, tell me all about these manifestations.

17. *katham̐ vidyām aham̐ yogim̐s*
tvām̐ sadā paricintayan
keṣu keṣu ca bhāveṣu
cintyo' si bhagavan mayā

18. *vistareṇātmano yogam̐*
vibhūtim̐ ca janārdana
bhūyaḥ kathaya tṛptir hi
śṛṇvato nāsti me' mṛtam

Śrī Bhagavān uvāca

19. *hanta te kathayiṣyāmi*
divyā hy ātma-vibhūtayaḥ
prādhānyataḥ kuru-śreṣṭha
nāsty anto vistarasya me

20. *aham ātmā guḍākeśa*
sarva-bhūtāśaya-sthitaḥ
aham ādiś ca madhyam̐ ca
bhūtānam anta eva ca

21. *ādityānām aham̐ viṣṇur*
jyotiṣām̐ ravir am̐śumān
marīcir marutām asmi
nakṣatrāṇam aham̐ śaśī

22. *vedānām̐ sāma-vedo' smi*
devānām asmi vāsavaḥ
indriyāṇām̐ manaś cāsmi
bhūtānām asmi cetanā

17. O Supreme mystic, how shall I know you? And in what manner of being shall I think of You? And how can You be always remembered by me?

18. Tell me again in detail of Your mystic power and opulences, O Krishna. I am never tired of listening to Your immortal words.

The Lord said:

19. To you Arjuna, I will tell of My divine manifestations, but only the essential parts, for the details of My opulences are endless.

20. I am the Soul present in all beings. I am also the beginning, middle, and end of all beings, Arjuna.

21. Of the Adityas, gods of the heavenly spheres,
I am Lord Vishnu.
Of lights, the radiant Sun.
Of Maruts, wind and storms,
I am Marici, their lord.
Of stars
I am the Moon.

22. Of Vedas, sacred knowledge,
I am the Sama Veda.
Of demigods
I am Vasavah, the king of heaven.
Of senses
I am the mind.
And in living beings
I am consciousness.

23. *rudrāṇām śaṅkaras cāsmi*
vitteśo yakṣa-rakṣasām
vasūnāṁ pāvakaś cāsmi
meruḥ śikhariṇām aham

24. *purodhasāṁ ca mukhyaṁ māṁ*
viddhi pārtha bṛhaspatim
senānīnām ahaṁ skandaḥ
sarasām asmi sāgaraḥ

25. *maharṣīṇāṁ bhṛgur ahaṁ*
girām asmy ekam akṣaram
yajñānāṃ japa-yajño' smi
sthāvarāṇāṁ himālayaḥ

26. *aśvatthaḥ sarva-vṛkṣāṇāṁ*
devarṣīṇāṁ ca nāradaḥ
gandharvāṇāṁ citrarathaḥ
siddhānāṁ kapilo muniḥ

27. *uccaiḥśravasam aśvānāṁ*
viddhi mām amṛtodbhavam
airāvataṁ gajendrāṇāṁ
narāṇāṁ ca narādhipam

23. Of the Rudras, terrifying gods,
I am Siva.
Of the Yakshas and Rakshasas, fiends and imps,
I am Kuvera, lord of wealth.
Of the Vasus, radiant gods,
I am Pavaka, god of fire.
And of mountain peaks
I am Meru, the fabulous residence of Brahma.

24. Know Me, Arjuna
Of priests
As Brihaspati, chief offerer of prayers and sacrifices.
Of generals
Skanda, god of war.
Of great waters
The ocean.

25. Of the great sages
I am Bhrigu, of the mystical race of beings.
Of words
I am the sacred monosyllable Om.
Of spiritual sacrifices
I am the muttered prayers.
Of immovable things
The Himalayas.

26. Of all trees, the holy fig tree.
Of divine sages, Narada,
messenger between God and humanity.
Of celestial musicians, Citraratha, their chief.
Of perfected beings, the ancient sage Kapila.

27. Of horses
Know Me as Ucchaihsrava, one of horses of the Sungod.
Of elephants
Airavata, the most excellent elephant of Indra.
Of men, the king.

28. *āyudhānām ahaṁ vajraṁ*
dhenūnām asmi kāmadhuk
prajanaś cāsmi kandarpaḥ
sarpāṇām asmi vāsukiḥ

29. *anantaś cāsmi nāgānāṁ*
varuṇo yādasām aham
pitṝṇām aryamā cāsmi
yamaḥ saṁyamatām aham

30. *prahlādaś cāsmi daityānāṁ*
kālaḥ kalayatām aham
mṛgāṇāṁ ca mṛgendro' haṁ
vainateyaś ca pakṣiṇām

31. *pavanaḥ pavatām asmi*
rāmaḥ śastra-bhṛtām aham
jhaṣāṇāṁ makaraś cāsmi
srotasām asmi jāhnavī

32. *sargāṇām ādir antaś ca*
madhyaṁ caivāham arjuna
adhyātma-vidyā vidyānāṁ
vādaḥ pravadatām aham

28. Of weapons
I am Indra's thunderbolt
Of cows
I am Kamadhuk, the heavenly cow of plenty.
For procreation
I am Kandarpah, the god of love.
Of serpents
I am Vasuki, the serpent-king.

29. Of watersnakes
I am Ananta, the snake-god.
Of acquatic beings
I am Varuna, the king.
Of ancestral spirits
I am Aryaman, the chief.
Of regulators
I am Yama, the God of death.

30. Of the Daityas, demons,
I am Prahlada, the pious son of demon Hiranyakasipu.
Of reckoners I am time.
Of forest animals
I am the lion.
And of birds
I am Vinata, Garuda, chief of the feathered race.

31. Of purifiers
I am the wind.
Of warriors
I am Lord Rama.
Of fishes
I am Maraka, the shark.
And of rivers
I am the Ganges.

32. Of all wordly creations, Arjuna
I am the beginning, middle, and end
Of all knowledge.
I am knowledge of the Supreme Spirit.
Of arguments
I am the natural conclusion.

33. *akṣarāṇām akāro' smi*
dvandvaḥ sāmāsikasya ca
aham evākṣayaḥ kālo
dhātāhaṁ viśvato-mukhaḥ

34. *mṛtyuḥ sarva-haraś cāham*
udbhavaś ca bhaviṣyatām
kīrtiḥ śrīr vāk ca nārīṇāṁ
smṛtir medhā dhṛtiḥ kṣamā

35. *bṛhat-sāma tathā sāmnāṁ*
gāyatrī chandasām aham
māsānāṁ mārga-śīrṣo' ham
ṛtūnāṁ kusumākaraḥ

36. *dyūtaṁ chalayatām asmi*
tejas tejasvinām aham
jayo' smi vyavasāyo' smi
sattvaṁ sattvavatām aham

37. *vṛṣṇīnaṁ vāsudevo' smi*
pāṇḍavānāṁ dhanañjayaḥ
munīnām apy ahaṁ vyāsaḥ
kavīnām uśanā kaviḥ

33. Of letters
I am the first letter, A.
Of dual compounds
I am the pair of opposites.
I am imperishable time
And I am also the creator Brahma whose face is turned in every direction.

34. I am all-destroying death.
I am existence and all which is to exist in the future.
Of feminine words
I am fame, glory, speech, memory, wisdom,
Resolution and patience.

35. Of the Saman hymns
I am the Brihat-saman, the most
clear-cut, emphatic, enchanting hymn.
Of the sacred texts of Vedic hymns
I am Gayatri, that which saves when repeated.
I am the first of months, Margasirsa, November - December.
And of seasons I am Spring.

36. In gambling
I am trickery.
I am the splendour of the splendid.
I am victory,
I am adventure,
I am the strength of the strong.

37. Of the Vrishnis
I am Vasudeva, Lord Krishna.
Of the Pandavas
I am Arjuna.
Of the celestial sages
I am Vyasa, compiler of the Vedas.
Of great thinkers
I am the seer Usana, descendent of Kavi.

38. *daṇḍo damayatām asmi*
nītir asmi jigīṣatām
maunaṁ caivāsmi guhyānāṁ
jñānaṁ jñānavatām aham

39. *yac cāpi sarva-bhūtānāṁ*
bījaṁ tad aham arjuna
na tad asti vinā yat syān
mayā bhūtaṁ carācaram

40. *nānto' sti mama divyānāṁ*
vibhūtīnāṁ paramtapa
eṣa tūddeśataḥ prokto
vibhuter vistaro mayā

41. *yad yad vibhūtimat sattvaṁ*
śrīmad ūrjitam eva vā
tat tad evāvagaccha tvaṁ
mama tejo-'ṁśa-sambhavam

42. *atha vā bahunaitena*
kiṁ jñātena tavārjuna
viṣṭabhyāham idaṁ kṛtsnam
ekāṁśena sthito jagat

38. Of law enforcers I am the rod of punishment.
Of those who desire victory
I am political science.
Of secrets
I am silence.
And I am the wisdom of the wise.

39. I am the seed of all beings Arjuna. Nothing animate or inanimate can exist without Me.

40. There is no end to My divine manifestations,
O destroyer of enemies.
This is only a brief explanation of My endless glories.

41. Know this—wherever glory, power, or fortune, reside, it originates from only a very small part of My splendour.

42. But what need is there, Arjuna, of all this detailed knowledge? With a single part of Myself I protect and support this entire world.

Chapter Eleven

The Universal Form

To fulfil Arjuna's desire Krishna gives him divine eyes to see His universal form. Arjuna then sees a fearsome form without beginning or end, within which are all things, all the demigods, all the fleeing demons and all the soldiers dieing in battle. The form is ferocious and terrifying and Arjuna pays his homage and requests to see again the Lord's gentle, two-armed form.

Arjuna uvāca

1. *mad-anugrahāya paramaṁ*
guhyam adhyātma-sañjñitam
yat tvayoktaṁ vacas tena
moho' yaṁ vigato mama

2. *bhavāpyayau hi bhūtānāṁ*
śrutau vistaraśo mayā
tvattaḥ kamala-pattrākṣa
māhātmyam api cāvyayam

3. *evam etad yathāttha tvam*
ātmānaṁ parameśvara
draṣṭum icchāmi te rūpam
aiśvaraṁ puruṣottama

4. *manyase yadi tac chakyaṁ*
mayā draṣṭum iti prabho
yogeśvara tato me tvaṁ
darśayātmānam avyayam

Śrī Bhagavān uvāca

5. *paśya me pārtha rūpāṇi*
śataśo' tha sahasraśaḥ
nānā-vidhāni divyāni
nānā-varṇākṛtīni ca

6. *paśyādityān vasūn rudrān*
aśvinau marutas tathā
bahūny adṛṣṭa-pūrvāṇi
paśyāścaryāṇi bhārata

Arjuna said:

1. You have graciously revealed these most excellent secrets concerning the self. Your words have dispelled my illusion.

2. From You, I have learnt in depth about the beginning and end of all living beings, and also of Your imperishable greatness.

3. As You declare to be the Supreme God Yourself, O Lord, I wish I could see your Supreme divine form.

4. O Lord, if You think it is possible for me to see You thus, then O Lord of mystic power, please reveal to me Your eternal Self.

The Lord said:

5. Behold Arjuna
My divine forms
In hundreds and thousands
Of various sorts, different shapes
And colours.

6. Behold the gods of heavenly spheres
The radiant gods
The terrifying gods
The celestial twins
The wind gods
And behold Bharata
Many wonders never seen before.

7. *ihaika-sthaṁ jagat kṛtsnaṁ*
paśyādya sa-carācaram
mama dehe guḍākeśa
yac cānyad draṣṭum icchasi

8. *na tu māṁ śakyase draṣṭum*
anenaiva sva-cakṣuṣā
divyaṁ dadāmi te cakṣuḥ
paśya me yogam aiśvaram

Sañjaya uvāca

9. *evam uktvā tato rājan*
mahā-yogeśvaro hariḥ
darśayām āsa pārhāya
paramaṁ rūpam aiśvaram

10. *aneka-vaktra-nayanam*
anekādbhuta-darśanam
aneka-divyābharaṇaṁ
divyānekodyatāyudham

11. *divya-mālyāmbara-dharaṁ*
divya-gandhānulepanam
sarvāścarya-mayaṁ devam
anantaṁ viśvato-mukham

12. *divi sūrya-sahasrasya*
bhaved yugapad utthitā
yadi bhāḥ sadṛśī sā syād
bhāsas tasya mahātmanaḥ

13. *tatraika-sthaṁ jagat kṛtsnaṁ*
pravibhaktam anekadhā
apaśyad deva-devasya
śarīre pāṇḍavas tadā

14. *tataḥ sa vismayāviṣṭo*
hṛṣṭa-romā dhanañjayaḥ
praṇamya śirasā devaṁ
kṛtāñjalir abhāṣata

7. Now, here, in My body, in one place, behold Arjuna the whole universe, the aggregate of all created things, animate, inanimate, and whatever else you wish to see.

8. But with these eyes you cannot see Me, therefore I give you divine eyes. Behold My supernatural power.

Sanjaya said:

9. Having so spoken, O King, the great Lord of mystic powers, Lord Krishna, revealed His supernatural form to Arjuna.

10. He saw many mouths and eyes, many wonderful sights, many divine ornaments, many uplifted weapons.

11. In celestial attire, wearing garlands anointed with divine fragrance, miraculous, shining, endless, facing all sides.

12. If the splendour of a thousand suns were to rise at once in the sky, their splendour would, perhaps, resemble the splendour of that great Lord.

13. There, at that time, Arjuna saw the whole universe, although divided in many ways, yet standing in one place in the bodily frame of the God of gods.

14. Filled with astonishment, thrilled with delight, Arjuna joined the palms of his hands, bowed his head in obeisance to the Supreme God.

Arjuna uvāca

15. *paśyāmi devāms tava deva dehe*
sarvāṁs tathā bhūta-viśeṣa-saṅghan
brahmāṇam īśaṁ kamalāsana-stham
ṛṣīṁś ca sarvān uragāṁś ca divyān

16. *aneka-bāhūdara-vaktra-netraṁ*
paśyāmi tvāṁ sarvato' nanta-rūpam
nāntaṁ na madhyaṁ na punas tavādiṁ
paśyami viśveśvara viśva-rūpa

17. *kirīṭinaṁ gadinaṁ cakriṇaṁ ca*
tejo-rāśiṁ sarvato dīptimantam
paśyāmi tvāṁ durnirīkṣyaṁ samantād
dīptānalārka-dyutim aprameyam

18. *tvam aksaraṁ paramaṁ veditavyaṁ*
tvam asya viśvasya paraṁ nidhānam
tvam avyayaṝ śāśvata-dharma-goptā
sanātanas tvaṁ puruṣo mato me

19. *anādi-madhyāntam ananta-vīryam*
ananta-bāhuṁ śaśi-sūrya-netram
paśyāmi tvāṁ dīpta-hutāśa-vaktraṁ
sva-tejasā viśvam idaṁ tapantam

20. *dyāv ā-pṛthivyor idam antaraṁ hi*
vyāptaṁ tvayaikena diśaś ca sarvāḥ
dṛṣṭvādbhutaṁ rūpam ugraṁ tavedaṁ
loka-trayaṁ pravyathitaṁ mahātman

21. *amī hi tvāṁ sura-saṅghā viśanti*
kecid bhītāḥ prāñjalayo gṛṇanti
svastīty uktvā maharṣi-siddha-sanghāḥ
stuvanti tvāṁ stutibhiḥ puṣkalābhiḥ

Arjuna said:

15. I see all the demigods in Your body; Lord Brahma on his lotus seat, Lord Siva, various kinds of beings, all the sages and celestial serpents.

16. I see Your cosmic form everywhere
With countless arms, stomachs, mouths, eyes.
I see Your innumerable forms
With no end, no middle, no beginning,
O Lord of the universe!

17. I see You with diadem, mace, discus; a radiant splendour shining everywhere, difficult to be seen, blazing like fire and sun on all sides, unfathomable!

18. You are to be known as the Supreme being, the imperishable. You are the highest residence of this universe. You are the undecaying guardian of eternal virtue. So I believe.

19. You are without beginning, middle, or end, of infinite power and countless arms. The Moon and Sun are Your eyes. I see the burning fire of oblation in Your mouth. Your radiance warms this universe.

20. You alone pervade all the regions of heaven and Earth and the space between, O sovereign Lord. Beholding Your supernatural and mighty form, the three worlds tremble with fear!

21. The assembly of demigods are entering into You. Some, out of fear, are offering prayers with joined palms. The assembly of perfected beings and sages are greeting and praising You with excellent hymns.

22. *rudrādityā vasavo ye ca sāḍhyā*
viśve' svinau marutaś coṣmapāś ca
gandharva-yakṣāsura-siddha-sanghā
vīkṣante tvāṁ vismitāś caiva sarve

23. *rūpaṁ mahat te baḥu-vaktra-netraṁ*
mahā-bāho bahu-bāhūru-pādam
bahūdaraṁ bahu-daṁṣṭrā-karālaṁ
dṛṣṭvā lokāḥ pravyathitās tathāham

24. *nabhah-spṛśaṁ dīptam aneka-varṇaṁ*
vyāttānanaṁ dīpta-viśala-netram
dṛṣṭvā hi tvāṁ pravyathitāntar-ātmā
dhṛtiṁ na vindāmi śamaṁ ca viṣṇo

25. *daṁṣṭrā-karālāni ca te mukhāni*
dṛṣṭvaiva kālānala-sannibhāni
diśo na jāne na labhe ca śarma
praṣīda deveśa jagan-nivāsa

26. *amī ca tvāṁ dhṛtarāṣṭrasya putrāḥ*
sarve sahaivāvani-pāla-saṅghaiḥ
bhīṣmo droṇaḥ sūta-putras tathāsau
sahasmadīyair api yodha-mukhyaiḥ

27. *vaktrāṇi te tvaramāṇā viśanti*
daṁṣṭrā-karālāni bhayānakāni
kecid vilagnā daśanāntareṣu
samdṛśyante cūrṇitair uttamāṅgaiḥ

28. *yathā nadīnāṁ bahavo' mbu-vegāḥ*
samudram evābhimukhā dravanti
tathā tavāmī nara-loka-vīrā
viśanti vaktrāṇy abhivijvalanti

29. *yathā pradīptaṁ jvalanaṁ pataṅgā*
viśanti nāśāya samṛddha-vegāḥ
tathaiva nāśāya viśanti lokās
tavāpi vaktrāṇi samṛddha-vegāḥ

22. The terrifying gods, the gods of the heavenly spheres, the radiant gods and the celestial beings, the celestial twins, the wind-gods, the paternal ancestors and the assembly of celestial musicians, good spirits, perfected sages and demons — all are looking on You in wonder.

23. Seeing Your mighty form
Of many mouths and eyes
Of many legs and feet
Of many stomachs, terrible tusks
O Lord, the worlds are frightened, as am I.

24. Seeing You touching the sky, glowing with various colours, with gaping mouths, large blazing eyes, O Lord Vishnu, I am frightened at heart. I can find neither courage nor peace.

25. Your terrible tusks and mouths resemble the world on fire. Looking at them, I find neither sense of direction nor peace. O Lord of gods, O abode of the universe, please be merciful to me.

26-27. The sons of Dhritarashtra, a host of kings, Bhishma, Drona, Karna, together with our own chief warriors are speedily entering Your terrible, tusked mouths. It is so dreadful to behold. Some are stuck with their heads smashed between Your teeth.

28. As the water of the rivers flows into the sea, so these wordly heroes enter into Your flaming mouths.

29. As moths, hastening towards death, enter the blazing fire, so the world of beings enters into Your mouths.

30 *lelihyase grasamānaḥ samantāl*
lokān samagrān vadanair jvaladbhiḥ
tejobhir āpūrya jagat samagraṁ
bhāsas tavogrāḥ pratapanti viṣṇo

31. *ākhyāhi me ko bhavān ugra-rūpo*
namo' stu te deva-vara prasīda
vijñātum icchāmi bhavantam ādyaṁ
na hi prajānāmi tava pravṛttim

Śrī Bhagavān uvāca

32. *kālo' smi loka-kṣaya-kṛi pravṛddho*
lokān samāhartum iha pravṛttaḥ
ṛte' pi tvāṁ na bhaviṣyanti sarve
ye' vasthitāḥ pratyanīkeṣu yodhāḥ

33. *tasmāt tvam uttiṣṭha yaśo labhasva*
jitvā śatrūn bhuṅkṣva rājyaṁ samṛddham
mayaivaite nihatāḥ pūrvam eva
nimitta-mātraṁ bhava savya-sācin

34. *droṇaṁ ca bhīṣmaṁ ca jayadrathaṁ ca*
karṇaṁ tathānyān api yodha-vīrān
mayā hatāṁs tvaṁ jahi mā vyathiṣṭhā
yudhyasva jetāsi raṇe sapatnān

Sañjaya uvāca

35. *etac chrutvā vacanaṁ keśavasya*
kṛtāñjalir vepamānaḥ kirītī
namaskṛtvā bhūya evāha kṛṣṇaṁ
sa-gadgadaṁ bhīta-bhītaī praṇamya

Arjuna uvāca

36. *sthāne hrsīkeśa tava prakīrtyā*
jagat prahṛṣyaty anurajyate ca
rakṣāṁsi bhītāni diśo dravanti
sarve namasyanti ca siddha-sanghāḥ

30. Devouring and licking the worlds from every side with Your flaming mouths, filling the whole universe with radiance, Your formidable splendour is tormenting, O Lord Vishnu.

31. Glory to You, O Supreme deity with such a terrible form, tell me, who You are? I want to know You. Surely, You are the primeval Lord. I do not understand Your manifestation. Please be merciful to me.

The Lord said:

32. I am mighty time that destroys the world. I have come here to destroy all people. Even without you, all these warriors standing on opposite sides shall die.

33. Rise, therefore, conquer your enemies, win glory, and enjoy a prosperous empire. These enemies have already been slain by Me. Just be the cause, O ambidextrous bowman.

34. Do not waver. Fight and kill. You will conquer your adversaries in battle for I have already slain Drona, Bhishma, Jayadratha, Karna and the other brave warriors.

Sanjaya said:

35. Listening to Krishna's words, a trembling and frightened Arjuna bowed with joined palms and paid homage to the Lord. He spoke to Him again in a hesitant voice.

Arjuna said:

36. The world is rightly devoted and delights in Your praise, O Lord of the senses. In fear, the demons flee in all directions, but the assembly of perfected beings bow down to You.

37. *kasmāc ca te nameran mahātman*
garīyase brahmano' py ādi-kartre
ananta deveśa jagan-nivāsa
tvam akṣaram sad asat tat paraṁ yat

38. *tvam ādi-devaḥ puruṣaḥ purāṇas*
tvam asya viśvasya paraṁ nidhānam
vettāsi vedyaṁ ca paraṁ ca dhāma
tvayā tataṁ viśvam ananta-rūpa

39. *vāyur yamo' gnir varuṇaḥ śaśāṅkaḥ*
prajāpatis tvaṁ prapitāmahaś ca
namo namas te' stu sahasra-kṛtvaḥ
punaś ca bhūyo' pi namo namas te

40. *namaḥ purastād atha pṛṣṭhatas te*
namo' stu te sarvata eva sarva
ananta-vīryāmita-vikramas tvaṁ
sarvaṁ samapnoṣi tato' si sarvaḥ

41. *sakheti matvā prasabhaṁ yad uktaṁ*
he kṛṣṇa he yādava he sakheti
ajānatā mahimānaṁ tavedaṁ
mayā pramādāt praṇayena vāpi

42. *yac cāvahāsārtham asat kṛto' si*
vihāra-śayyāsana-bhojaneṣu
eko' thavāpy acyuta tat-samakṣaṁ
tat kṣāmaye tvām aham aprameyam

43. *pitāsi lokasya carācarasya*
tvam asya pūjyaś ca gurur garīyān
na tvat-samo' sty abhyadhikaḥ kuto' nyo
loka-traye' py apratima-prabhāva

44. *tasmāt praṇamya praṇidhāya kāyaṁ*
prasādaye tvām aham īśam īḍyam
piteva putrasya sakheva sakhyuḥ
priyah priyāyarhasi deva soḍhum

37. And why should they not bow to you, O Supreme soul. You are the first creator, greater than Brahma. O eternal Lord of gods, abode of the universe, You are existence and non-existence. You are the most high.

38. You are the original God, the most ancient Supreme Being. You are the highest place of refuge, the knower and that which is to be known. You are the shelter of the demigods. You pervade the entire universe, O being of innumerable forms.

39. You are the God of wind, ocean, fire and death. You are the Moon and Lord of all creatures. You are the great-grandfather. Let there be salutations to You a thousand times, and again and again!

40. Salutations to You from everywhere, before You and behind You. O Lord, You are everything, immense in strength, boundless in valour. You fulfil all, therefore You are all.

41. Thinking of You as a mere friend I might have, in the past, imprudently or carelessly called You, "O Krishna," "O Yadhava," "My dear friend," unaware of Your glories.

42. In whatever way I have offended You, while joking, in pastimes, during meals, while resting, sitting among friends or alone, O imperishable Krishna, I beg You to forgive me.

43. You are the father of the world with all its aggregate of created things, whether animate or inanimate. You are the most venerable and respectable spiritual preceptor. In all the three worlds, no one is on the same level as You. How could there be anyone more powerful than You, O incomparable Lord?

44. Therefore, I bow down and prostrate myself to beg mercy O praiseworthy Lord, be gracious. Please be patient with me, as a father with his son, a friend with his friend, a lover with his beloved.

45. *adṛṣṭa-pūrvaṁ hṛṣito' smi dṛṣṭvā*
bhayena ca pravyathitaṁ mano me
tad eva me darśaya deva rūpaṁ
prasīda deveśa jagan-nivāsa

46. *kirīṭinaṁ gadinaṁ cakra-hastam*
icchāmi tvāṁ draṣṭum ahaṁ tathaiva
tenaiva rūpeṇa catur-bhujena
sahasra-bāho bhava viśva-mūrte

Śrī Bhagavān uvāca

47. *mayā prasannema tavārjunedam*
rūpaṁ paraṁ darśitam ātma-yogāt
tejo-mayam viśvam anantam ādyaṁ
yan me tvad anyena na dṛṣṭa-pūrvam

48. *na veda-yajñādhyayanair na dānair*
na ca kriyābhir na tapobhir ugraiḥ
evaṁ-rūpaḥ śakya ahaṁ nṛ-loke
draṣṭuṁ tvad anyena kuru pravīra

49. *mā te vyathā mā ca vimūḍha-bhāvo*
dṛṣṭvā rūpaṁ ghoram idṛṅ mamedam
vyapeta-bhīḥ prīta-manāḥ punas tvaṁ
tad eva me rūpam idaṁ prapaśya

Sañjaya uvāca

50. *ity arjunaṁ vāsudevas tathoktvā*
svakaṁ rūpaṁ darśayām āsa bhūyaḥ
āśvāsayām āsa ca bhītaṁ enaṁ
bhūtvā punaḥ saumya-vapur mahātmā

Arjuna uvāca

51. *dṛṣṭvedaṁ mānuṣaṁ rūpaṁ*
tava saumyaṁ janārdana
idānim asmi samvṛttaḥ
sa-cetāḥ prakṛtiṁ gataḥ

45. I have seen what has never been seen before and I am thrilled with joy, yet fear grips my mind. O Lord, please show me Your usual form. Be so gracious, O world-abode, O Lord of gods.

46. O Supreme Spirit of a thousand arms, I only desire to see that form of Yours which is crowned, four-armed, with mace and discus in hand.

The Lord said:

47. Because I am pleased with you, Arjuna, I have shown you My supreme form by My own disposition. This resplendent, universal, eternal, primeval form has never been seen by anyone other than you.

48. Neither by Vedic study, spiritual sacrifice, charity, religious activities, nor by severe religious austerities, can the world of people see Me in such a form. Only you have seen this, O best of the Kurus.

49. Do not be afraid or perplexed having seen this dreadful form of Mine. Behold My usual form again. Now be free from fear and pleased in mind.

Sanjaya said:

50. Having spoken thus to Arjuna, Lord Krishna showed His own form again, and taking on this beautiful form, the Supreme Soul, comforted the terrified Arjuna.

Arjuna said:

51. Seeing Your gentle, human form, O Vishnu, I am now composed in mind and restored to my own nature.

Śrī Bhagavān uvāca

52. *su-durdarśam idaṁ rūpaṁ*
dṛṣṭavān asi yan mama
devā apy asya rūpasya
nityaṁ darśana-kāṅkṣiṇaḥ

53. *nāhaṁ vedair na tapasā*
na dānena na cejyayā
śakya evaṁ-vidho draṣṭuṁ
dṛṣṭavan asi māṁ yathā

54. *bhaktyā tv ananyayā śakya*
aham evaṁ-vidho' rjuna
jñātuṁ draṣṭuṁ ca tattvena
praveṣṭuṁ ca paramtapa

55. *mat-karma-kṛn mat-paramo*
mad-bhaktaḥ saṅga-varjitaḥ
nirvairaḥ sarva-bhūteṣu
yaḥ sa māṁ eti pāṇḍava

The Lord said:

52. This eternal form of Mine which you are now seeing, is indeed very difficult to see. Even the heavenly demigods are longing to see this form.

53. Neither by the sacred Vedas, nor religious austerity, nor charity, nor worship, am I to be seen in such a form as seen by you.

54. But through undistracted devotion Arjuna, I can, in reality, be seen, known and attained in this ordinary form, O destroyer of enemies.

55. One who works for Me, who looks on Me as the most high, who is devoted to Me, who is free from attachment and who bears no grudge to any living beings, comes to Me, Arjuna.

Chapter Twelve

Union with God Through Devotion

The Lord describes two paths to union with God, the impersonal and the devotional, but recommends the path of devotion. There are several alternatives for those who are unable, but He declares that the devotee is most dear to Him.

Arjuna uvāca

1. *evaṁ satata-yuktā ye*
bhaktās tvāṁ paryupāsate
ye cāpy akṣaram avyaktaṁ
teṣāṁ ke yoga-vittamāḥ

Śrī Bhagavān uvāca

2. *mayy āveśya mano ye māṁ*
nitya-yuktā upāsate
śraddhayā parayopetās
te me yuktatamā matāḥ

3. *ye tv akṣaram anirdeśyam*
avyaktaṁ paryupāsate
sarvatra-gam acintyaṁ ca
kūṭa-stham acalaṁ dhruvam

4. *sanniyamyendriya-grāmaṁ*
sarvatra sama-buddhayaḥ
te prāpnuvanti mām eva
sarva-bhūta-hite ratāḥ

5. *kleśo' dhikataras teṣām*
avyaktāsakta-cetasām
avyaktā hi gatir duḥkhaṁ
dehavadbhir avāpyate

6. *ye tu sarvāṇi karmāṇi*
mayi saṁnyasya mat-parāḥ
ananyenaiva yogena
māṁ dhyāyanta upāsate

7. *teṣām ahaṁ samuddhartā*
mṛtyu-saṁsāra-sāgarāt
bhavāmi na cirāt pārtha
mayy āveśita-cetasām

Arjuna said:

1. Who are the most perfect in *yoga,* those devotees who are constantly engaged in devotion to You, or those who worship the imperishable, unmanifest *brahman?*

The Lord said:

2. Those who are devoted to Me, who always concentrate their minds on Me, endowed with the highest trust, who worship Me, them, I consider to be the most perfect.

3-4. *Brahman* is unmanifest, imperishable, indefinable, omnipresent, inconceivable, unchangeable, immovable and eternal. Those who restrain their senses, who always respect all beings equally and engage themselves in their welfare, who worship *brahman,* they also reach Me.

5. For those who concentrate their minds on the unmanifest *brahman* their trouble is greater. It is very difficult for the embodied to reach the goal of the unmanifest *brahman.*

6-7. But those who regard Me as most high, who dedicate all activities to Me, whose minds are fixed on Me, who meditate and worship Me with *yoga* philosophy without deviation, them, O Arjuna, I very soon deliver from the ocean of the endless cycle of births and deaths.

8. *mayy eva mana ādhatsva*
mayi buddhiṁ niveśaya
nivasiṣyasi mayy eva
ata ūrdhvaṁ na saṁśayaḥ

9. *atha cittaṁ samādhātuṁ*
na śaknoṣi mayi sthiram
abhyāsa-yogena tato
mām icchāptuṁ dhanañjaya

10. *abhyāse' py asamartho' si*
mat-karma-paramo bhava
mad-artham api karmāṇi
kurvan siddhim avāpsyasi

11. *athaitad apy aśakto' si*
kartuṁ mad-yogam āśritaḥ
sarva-karma-phala-tyāgaṁ
tataḥ kuru yatātmavān

12. *śreyo hi jñānam abhyāsāj*
jñānād dhyānaṁ viśiṣyate
dhyānāt karma-phala-tyāgas
tyāgāc chāntir anantaram

13. *adveṣṭā sarva-bhūtānāṁ*
maitraḥ karuṇa eva ca
nirmamo nirahaṅkāraḥ
sama-duḥkha-sukhaḥ kṣamī

14. *samtuṣṭaḥ satataṁ yogī*
yatātmā dṛḍha-niścayaḥ
mayy arpita-mano-buddhir
yo mad-bhaktaḥ sa me priyaḥ

15. *yasmān nodvijate loko*
lokān nodvijate ca yaḥ
harṣāmarṣa-bhayodvegair
mukto yaḥ sa ca me priyaḥ

8. Concentrate your mind on Me. Turn your intelligence towards Me, and you will dwell in Me without doubt.

9. If you are unable to concentrate your mind constantly on Me, then, O winner of wealth, try to reach Me by the practice of frequent meditation.

10. If you are incapable of such a practice, then dedicate yourself to My work. You shall reach perfection by performing work for My sake.

11. If you are unable to do even this, then take shelter in devotion to Me. Renounce the fruits of all work and be self-restrained.

12. Knowledge, however, is better than religious practice, and meditation is better than knowledge. But the renunciation of the fruits of work excels meditation indeed, for such renunciation leads to peace thereafter.

13-14. My devotee is dear to Me who is friendly, compassionate, without hatred to any being, who is unselfish, forgiving, humble, equipoised in pain and pleasure, ever content, self-restrained, of firm conviction, steady in meditation and whose mind and intellect are fixed on Me.

15. One is also dear to Me who does not distress others, nor is disturbed by anyone, who is free from joy, anger, fear and anxiety.

16. *anapekṣaṇ śucir dakṣa*
udāsīno gata-vyathaḥ
sarvārambha-parityāgī
yo mad-bhaktaḥ sa me priyaḥ

17. *yo na hṛṣyati na dveṣṭi*
na śociati na kāṅkṣati
śubhāśubha-parityāgī
bhaktimān-yaḥ sa me priyaḥ

18. *samaḥ śatrau ca mitre ca*
tathā mānāpamānayoḥ
śītoṣṇa-sukha-duḥkheṣu
samaḥ sanga-vivarjitaḥ

19. *tulya-nindā-stutir maunī*
samtuṣṭo yenao kenacit
aniketaḥ sthira-matir
bhaktimān me priyo naraḥ

20. *ye tu dharmyāmṛtam idaṁ*
yathoktaṁ paryupāsate
śraddadhānā mat-paramā
bhaktās te' tīva me priyāḥ

16. My devotee is dear to Me who is carefree, honest, industrious, neutral, free from distress and who is renounced in all his undertakings.

17. My devotee is dear to Me who neither rejoices, nor hates, nor grieves and who renounces both good and evil things.

18-19. That person of devotion is dear to Me, who is just toward friend and foe; equal in honour and dishonour, cold and heat, pain and pleasure; free from worldly attachment, indifferent to praise and blame, always silent, content with anything; who has no home and has fixed determination.

20. Those devotees are very-very dear to Me, who engage with faith in this eternal path as described, regarding Me as the Supreme, the most high.

CHAPTER THIRTEEN

The Field, the Knower of the Field and Nature

Lord Krishna explains that the body is the field, the knower is the individual soul and Krishna dwelling within the heart, pervading all, is the knower in all fields. One can approach the Supreme understanding what is knowledge; how the soul and the Supreme soul can be perceived; what is nature, its qualities and transformation; and about cause and effect.

Arjuna uvaca

prakrtim purusam caiva
ksetram ksetra-jñam eva ca
etad veditum icchāmi
jñānaṁ jñeyaṁ ca keśava

Śrī Bhagavān uvāca

1. *idaṁ śarīraṁ kaunteya*
kṣetram ity abhidhīyate
etad yo vetti tam prāhuḥ
kṣetra-jña iti tad-vidaḥ

2. *kṣetra-jñaṁ cāpi māṁ viddhi*
sarva-kṣetreṣu bhārata
kṣetra-kṣetrajñayor jñānaṁ
yat taj jñānaṁ mataṁ mama

3. *tat kṣetraṁ yac ca yādṛk ca*
yad-vikāri yataś ca yat
sa ca yo yat-prabhāvaś ca
tat samāsena me śṛṇu

4. *ṛṣibhir bahudhā gītaṁ*
chandobhir vividhaiḥ pṛthak
brahma-sūtra-padaiś caiva
hetumadbhir viniścitaiḥ

5. *mahā-bhūtāny ahaṅkāro*
buddhir avyaktam eva ca
indriyāṇi daśaikaṁ ca
pañca cendriya-gocarāḥ

6. *icchā dveṣaḥ sukhaṁ duḥkhaṁ*
saṅghātaś cetanā dhṛtiḥ
etat kṣetraṁ samāsena
sa-vikāram udāhṛtam

Arjuna said:

O Lord, I wish to know about nature, the enjoyer, the field and the knower of the field, knowledge and what should be known.

The Lord said:

1. This body is called the field, Arjuna, and one who knows this field is called the knower of the field by those who know their true nature.

2. I am the knower in all fields, Bharata. To know the field and the knower of the field, I regard as knowledge.

3. Hear from Me in brief about the field, what it is, its nature, its origin, the knower and his powers.

4. Sages have, in many ways, repeatedly chanted of the knower and the field in sacred hymns, and in the well-founded Vedanta regarding cause and effect.

5-6. This is the field briefly declared with its undergoing modifications: the great elements, egoism, intellect and also the unmanifest, the ten senses, the mind and the five sense objects, desire, hatred, pleasure, pain, the aggregate of body and matter, consciousness, and convictions.

7. *amānitvam adambhitvam*
ahiṁsā kṣāntir ārjavam
ācāryopāsanaṁ śaucaṁ
sthairyam ātma-vinigrahaḥ

8. *indriyārtheṣu vairāgyam*
anahankāra eva ca
janma-mṛtyu-jarā-vyādhi
duḥkha-doṣānudarśanam

9. *asaktir anabhiṣvaṅgaḥ*
putra-dāra-gṛahādiṣu
nityaṁ ca sama-cittatvam
iṣṭāniṣṭopapattiṣu

10. *mayi cānanya-yogena*
bhaktir avyabhicāriṇī
vivkta-deśa-sevitvam
aratir jana-saṁsadi

11. *adhyatma-jñāna-nityatvaṁ*
tattva-jñānārtha-darśanam
etaj jñānam iti proktam
ajñānaṁ yad ato' nyathā

12. *jñeyaṁ yat tat pravakṣyāmi*
yaj jñātvamṛtam aśnute
anādi-mat-paraṁ brahma
na sat tan nāsad ucyate

13. *sarvataḥ pāṇi-pādaṁ tat*
sarvato'kṣi-śiro-mukham
sarvataḥ śrutimal loke
sarvam āvṛtya tiṣṭhati

14. *sarvendriya guṇābhāsaṁ*
sarvendriya-vivarjitam
asaktaṁ sarva-bhṛc caiva
nirguṇaṁ guṇa-bhoktṛ ca

7. Modesty, sincerity, non-violence, forgiveness, honesty, serving a spiritual preceptor, purity of mind, fixity of faith and self-control.

8. Freedom from pride, freedom from worldly desires and sense-objects. To be aware of the inconvenience of birth, death, old age, disease and distress.

9. Detachment from wordly feelings. Detachment from wife, son, home, etc. Constant equanimity towards any desired or undesired thing.

10. Unfailing devotion to Me through undistracted spiritual practices. Unattachment to people in general in order to seek solitary places.

11. Constancy in knowledge of the Supreme Spirit and to consider knowledge of the Truth as real wealth. All these I declare to be knowledge; anything contrary is ignorance.

12. I will explain to you what must be known. When you know it, you will reach the world of immortals. It has no beginning. It is the most high. It is God. He is known to be neither existent nor inexistent.

13. He has hands and feet everywhere; eyes, heads, and mouths everywhere; ears everywhere. He continuously pervades everything.

14. He seems to have human qualities and senses, yet He is exempt from them. Although exempt from qualities, yet He experiences them. He is unattached, yet He sustains all.

15. *bahir antaś ca bhūtānām*
acaraṁ caram eva ca
sūkṣmatvāt tad avijñeyaṁ
dūra-sthaṁ cāntike ca tat

16. *avibhaktaṁ ca bhūteṣu*
vibhaktam iva ca sthitam
bhūta-bhartṛ ca taj jñeyaṁ
grasiṣṇu prabhaviṣṇu ca

17. *jyotiṣām api taj jyotis*
tamasaḥ param ucyate
jñānaṁ jñeyaṁ jñāna-gamyaṁ
hṛdi sarvasya viṣṭhitam

18. *iti kṣetraṁ tathā jñānaṁ*
jñeyaṁ coktaṁ samāsataḥ
mad-bhakta etad vijñāya
mad-bhāvāyopapadyate

19. *prakṛtiṁ puruṣaṁ caiva*
viddhy anādī ubhāv api
vikārāṁś ca guṇāṁś caiva
viddhi prakṛti-sambhavān

20. *kārya-karaṇa-kartṛtve*
hetuḥ prakṛtir ucyate
puruṣaḥ sukha-duḥkhānāṁ
bhoktṛtve hetur ucyate

21. *puruṣaḥ prakṛti-stho hi*
bhuṅkte prakṛti-jān guṇān-
kāraṇaṁ guṇa-saṅgo' sya
sad-asad-yoni-janmasu

22. *upadraṣṭānumantā ca*
bhartā bhoktā maheśvaraḥ
paramātmeti cāpy ukto
dehe' smin puruṣaḥ paraḥ

15. His presence is subtle and thus He remains inside and outside of all that exists, both movable and immovable. He is undiscernible. Although very far away, yet He is so near.

16. He appears divided among all that exist, yet He is undivided. It should be known that He is the Lord of all beings. He creates and He destroys.

17. He is the light of lights. He is beyond darkness. He is knowledge and that which should be known. He is the goal of knowledge. He dwells in everybody's heart.

18. I have spoken briefly about the field, knowledge and what should be known. My devotee recognising this, enters into My nature.

19. It should be understood that both the material world and the Supreme Being have no beginning. It should also be understood that the transformations and qualities of all existing beings arise from the material world.

20. For cause and effect of deeds, the material world is said to be the cause. In the experience of joy and sorrow, the human being is said to be the cause.

21. The human being, living in the material world, enjoys its qualities. Attachment to the material qualities is the cause of good or evil birth.

22. Yet also in this material body, is the Supreme Who is the witness. He approves, sustains and experiences. He is the Universal Soul and is also called the Supreme Being.

23. *ya evaṁ vetti puruṣaṁ*
prakṛtiṁ ca guṇaiḥ saha
sarvathā vartamāno' pi
na sa bhūyo' bhijāyate

24. *dhyānenātmani paśyanti*
kecid ātmānam ātmanā
anye sāṅkhyena yogena
karma-yogena cāpare

25. *anye tv evam ajānantaḥ*
śrutvānyebhya upāsate
te'pi cātitaranty eva
mṛtyuṁ śruti-parāyaṇāḥ

26. *yāvat sañjāyate kiñcit*
sattvaṁ sthāvara-jaṅgamam
kṣetra-kṣetrajña-saṁyogāt
tad viddhi bharatarṣabha

27. *samaṁ sarveṣu bhūteṣu*
tiṣṭhantaṁ parameśvaram
vinaśyatsv avinaśyantaṁ
yaḥ paśyati sa paśyati

28. *samaṁ paśyan hi sarvatra*
samavasthitam īśvaram
na hinasty ātmanātmānaṁ
tato yāti parāṁ gatim

29. *prakṛtyaiva ca karmāṇi*
kriyamāṇāni sarvaśaḥ
yaḥ paśyati tathātmānam
akartāraṁ sa paśyati

3. *yadā bhūta-pṛthag-bhāvam*
eka-stham anupaśyati
tata eva ca vistāraṁ
brahma saṁpadyate tadā

23. One who knows God, the material world and its human qualities, will not be reborn no matter what one's present life may be.

24. Some perceive God in the self, by the self, through profound religious meditation, some through spiritual knowledge, some through religious duties.

25. But others, although devoid of spiritual knowledge, hearing what is the supreme refuge from others, begin worshipping Him and overcome death.

26. Whatever being is born, movable or immovable, is born from the union of the field and the knower of the field, know that, O Prince.

27. One who perceives the Supreme Lord situated alike in all beings, and the imperishable in the perishable, truly perceives.

28. When one perceives the Supreme Lord, situated everywhere alike, then one's mind is no longer in conflict with oneself and one attains the highest goal.

29. All activities are performed by material nature. Nothing is performed by the individual self. One who perceives this truly sees.

30. When one perceives that all living entities, although appearing to be separate identities, are situated in the One, and are expanded everywhere from that One alone, then one attains God.

31. *anāditvān nirguṇatvāt*
paramātmāyam āvyayaḥ
śarīra-stho' pi kaunteya
na karoti na lipyate

32. *yathā sarva-gataṁ saukṣ myād*
ākāśaṁ nopalipyate
sarvatrāvasthito dehe
tathātmā nopalipyate

33. *yathā prakāśayaty ekaḥ*
kṛtsnaṁ lokam imaṁ raviḥ
kṣetraṁ kṣetrī tathā kṛtsnaṁ
prakāśayati bhārata

34. *kṣetra-kṣetrajñayor evam*
antaraṁ jñāna-cakṣuṣā
bhūta-prakṛti-mokṣaṁ ca
ye vidur yānti te param

31. The imperishable soul is eternal, transcendental and beyond material nature. Although dwelling in the body it neither acts nor is affected, Arjuna.

32. Just as the sky pervades everywhere, yet is not mixed because of its subtlety, in like manner, the self never mixes though it pervades the whole body.

33. As the Sun alone illumines the entire universe, so the entire field is illuminated by the soul, O son of Bharata.

34. Those who perceive, with the eye of intelligence, the distinction between the body and the knower of the body, and the path of liberation from the material world, approach the Supreme.

Chapter Fourteen

The Three Qualities of Material Nature

Wisdom is first to understand the interactions of the three modes of material nature and how to overcome their influence. One can then become established in eternal truth and bliss.

Śrī Bhagavān uvāca

1. *paraṁ bhūyaḥ pravakṣyāmi*
jñānānāṁ jñānam uttamam
yaj jñātvā munayaḥ sarve
parāṁ siddhim ito gatāḥ

2. *idaṁ jñānam upāśritya*
mama sādharmyam āgatāḥ
sarge' pi nopajāyante
pralaye na vyathanti

3. *mama yonir mahad brahma*
tasmin garbhaṁ dadhāmy aham
sambhavaḥ sarva-bhūtānāṁ
tato bhavati bhārata

4. *sarva-yoniṣu kaunteya*
mūrtayaḥ sambhavanti yāḥ
tāsāṁ brahma mahad yonir
ahaṁ bīja-pradaḥ pitā

5. *sattvaṁ rajas tama iti*
guṇāḥ prakṛti-sambhavāḥ
nībadh nanti mahā-bāho
dehe dehinam avyayam

6. *tatra sattvaṁ nirmalavāt*
prakāśakam anāmayam
sukha-saṅgena badhnāti
jñāna-saṅgena cānagha

7. *rajo rāgātmakaṁ viddhi*
tṛṣṇā-saṅga-samudbhavam
tan nibadhnati kaunteya
karma-saṅgena dehinam

8. *tamas tv ajñāna-jaṁ viddhi*
mohanaṁ sarva-dehināṁ
pramādālasya-nidrābhis
tan nibadhnāti bhārata

The Lord said:

1. I shall again declare the highest knowledge of all wisdom, knowing which, the sages departing from this world reached the supreme perfection.

2. Those who rely on this knowledge attain My nature. They are neither born when the world is created nor disturbed when it is destroyed.

3. Brahma, the great creator, is My womb within which I place the seed making possible the birth of all beings, O Bharata.

4. Whatever species are born from any womb, O Kaunteya, their source of birth is the supreme womb, Brahma, and I am the seed-giving father.

5. Goodness, passion and ignorance, are human qualities born of the material world, O mighty-armed. They bind the imperishable soul in the body.

6. Because goodness is pure, it gives light and health. It also binds one to the desire for virtue and for knowledge, sinless one.

7. The quality of passion is composed of desire and yearning, son of Kunti. It is the source of worldly attachment and greed and binds people by their love for action.

8. Ignorance is born of darkness, Bharata. It deludes all people, binding them to negligence, laziness and sleep.

9. *sattvaṁ sukhe sañjayati*
rajaḥ karmaṇi bhārata
jñānam āvṛtya tu tamaḥ
pramāde sañjayaty uta

10. *rajas tamaś cābhibhūya*
sattvaṁ bhavati bhārata
rajaḥ sattvaṁ tamaś caiva
tamaḥ sattvaṁ rajastathā

11. *sarva-dvāreṣu dehe' smin*
prakāśa upajāyate
jñānaṁ yadā tadā vidyād
vivṛddhaṁ sattvam ity uta

12. *lobhaḥ pravṛttir ārambhaḥ*
karmaṇām aśamaḥ spṛhā
rajasy etāni jāyante
vivṛddhe bharatarṣabha

13. *aprakāśo pravṛttiś ca*
pramādo moha eva ca
tamasy etāni jāyante
vivṛddhe kuru-nandana

14. *yadā sattve pravṛddhe tu*
pralayaṁ yāti deha-bhṛt
tadottama-vidāṁ lokān
amalān pratipadyate

15. *rajasi pralayaṁ gatvā*
karma-saṅgiṣu jāyate
tathā pralīnas tamasi
mūḍha-yoniṣu jāyate

16. *karmaṇaḥ sukṛtasyāhuḥ*
sāttvikaṁ nirmalaṁ phalam
rajasas tu phalam duḥkham
ajñānaṁ tamasaḥ phalam

9. Goodness binds one to happiness, passion to action; but ignorance veils knowledge and binds one to forgetfulness, Bharata.

10. Goodness predominates over passion and ignorance; passion over goodness and ignorance; even ignorance over goodness and passion, Bharata.

11. When the light of knowledge illuminates all the gates of the body, then it should be known that goodness is indeed predominant.

12. When greed, activity, endeavour and uncontrollable desire are on the increase, then passion is predominant, O Prince.

13. When darkness, inactivity, negligence, and delusion arise, then ignorance is predominant, son of Kuru.

14. When goodness is predominant at the time of a person's death, then he reaches the pure world of the enlightened ones.

15. When passion is predominant at the time of a person's death, then he is born among those who are attached to action. When ignorance is predominant at the time of death, then he is born among the animal species.

16. It is said that goodness is the fruit of pure and virtuous deeds. Passion results in sorrow, and ignorance results in delusion.

17. *sattvāt sañjāyate jñānaṁ*
rajaso lobha eva ca
pramāda-mohau tamaso
bhavato' jñānam eva ca

18. *ūrdhvaṁ gacchanti sattva-sthā*
madhye tiṣṭhanti rājasāḥ
jaghanya-guṇa-vṛtti-sthā
adho gacchanti tāmasāḥ

19. *nānyaṁ guṇebhyaḥ kartāraṁ*
yadā draṣṭānupaśyati
guṇebhyaś ca paraṁ vetti
mad bhāvaṁ so' dhigacchati

20. *guṇān etān atītya trīn*
dehī deha-samudbhavān
janma-mṛtyu-jara-duḥkhair
vimukto' mṛtam aśnute

Arjuna uvāca

21. *kair lingais trīn guṅān etān*
atīto bhavati prabho
kim-ācāraḥ kathaṁ caitāṁs
trīn guṇān ativartate

Śrī Bhagavān uvāca

22. *prakāśaṁ ca pravṛttiṁ ca*
moham eva ca pāṇḍava
na dveṣṭi sampravṛttāni
na nivṛttāni kāṅkṣati

23. *udāsīna-vad āsīno*
gunair yo na vicālyate
guṇā vartanta ity evam
yo'vatiṣṭhati neṅgate

17. From goodness arises knowledge; from passion greed; from ignorance arises negligence, illusion and foolishness.

18. Those in goodness go to higher realms. Those in passion remain in the middle planes, while those in ignorance, with the lowest qualities, go down.

19. When a person, perceives no other performer in all activities than the qualities of nature, and knows that higher than these qualities is God, he enters My essence.

20. The material body evolves from the three *gunas,* qualities. When a person overcomes them, he is exempt from birth, death, old age and sorrows and gains immortality.

Arjuna said:

22. What are the characteristics of a person, Lord, who has overcome the three qualities? How does such a person behave? And how does he overcome these three qualities?

The Lord said:

23. One who does not hate spiritual illumination, activity or delusions when they arise, son of Pandu, nor desires them, when they are gone.

24. One who remains neutral although situated in the material qualities, and is not agitated, knowing it is but the qualities reacting, and remains firm and determined.

24. *sama-duḥkha-sukhaḥ sva-sthaḥ*
sama-loṣṭāśma-kāñcannaḥ
tulya-priyāpriyo dhīras
tulya-nindātma-saṁstutiḥ

25. *mānāpamānayos tulyas*
tulyo mitrāri-pakṣayoḥ
sarvārambha-parityāgī
guṇātītaḥ sa ucyate

26. *māṁ ca yo'vyabhicāreṇa*
bhakti-yogena sevate
sa guṇān samatītyaitān
brahma-bhūyāya kalpate

27. *brahmaṇo hi pratiṣṭhāham*
amṛtasyāvyayasya ca
śāśvatasya ca dharmasya
sukhasyaikāntikasya ca

25. One who is resolute, self-abiding, indifferent to pleasure and pain, pleasant and unpleasant things, praise and blame; to whom a clod of earth, a stone and a piece of gold are alike.

26. One who is indifferent to honour and dishonour, friend and foe, and who has renounced all undertakings. Such a person is said to have overcome the qualities of nature.

27. One who constantly serves Me with loving devotion overcomes these *gunas,* qualities, and is elevated to *brahman.*

28. I am the foundation of the immortal, imperishable *brahman,* everlasting truth and absolute bliss.

CHAPTER FIFTEEN

The Secrets of the Supreme

The universe is described as a great tree of entanglement which needs to be cut down with the axe of detachment. The living entities struggle with the material senses but the Supreme is present in everything, and perceiving this one's endeavours can become perfect.

Śri Bhagavān uvāca

1. *ūrdhva-mūlam adhaḥ-śākham*
aśvatthaṁ prāhur avyayam
chandāṁsi yasya parṇāni
yas taṁ veda sa veda-vit

2. *adhaś cordhvaṁ prasṛtās tasya śākhā*
guṇa-pravṛddhā viṣaya-pravālaḥ
adhaś ca mūlāny anusamtatāni
karmānubandhīni manuṣya-loke

3. *na rūpam asyeha tathopalabhyate*
nānto na cādir na ca sampratiṣṭhā
aśvattham enaṁ su-virūḍha-mūlam
asaṅga-śastreṇa dṛḍhena chittvā

4. *tataḥ padaṁ tat parimārgitavyaṁ*
yasmin gatā na nivartanti bhūyaḥ
tam eva cādyaṁ purusam pradadye
yataḥ pravṛttiḥ prasṛtā purāṇī

5. *nirmāna-mohā jita-saṅga-doṣā*
adhyātma-nityā vinivṛtta-kāmāḥ
dvandvair vimuktāḥ sukha-duḥkha-sañjñair
gacchanty amūḍhāḥ padam avyayaṁ tat

6. *na tad bhāsayate sūryo*
na śaśāṅko na pāvakaḥ
yad gatvā na nivartante
tad dhāma paramaṁ mama

7. *mamaivāṁśo jīva-loke*
jīva-bhūtaḥ sanātanaḥ
manaḥ-ṣaṣṭhānīndriyāṇi
prakṛti-sthāni karṣati

8. *śarīraṁ yad avāpnoti*
yac cāpy utkrāmatīśvaraḥ
gṛhītvaitāni saṁyāti
vāyur gandhān ivāśayāt

The Lord said:

1. They say there is an eternal tree of creation, with its roots above and its branches below. The sacred texts of the Vedic hymns, are its leaves. One who knows this tree, knows the Vedas.

2. It spreads its branches above and below, nourished by the qualities of material nature. The young shoots are sense-objects that stretch down to the roots, resulting in fruitive activities in the world of men.

3. Its form as such cannot be perceived in this world, neither its end, its beginning, nor its foundation. This tree of creation is firmly rooted, but one must cut it down with the strong axe of detachment.

4. One must look for that place from which having reached one never returns. There one must take refuge in that primeval God from Whom everything has originated and extended since time began.

5. Free from arrogance and delusion
Overcoming the faults of worldly attachment
Constantly dwelling in the Supreme Spirit
Devoid of the dualities, known as pleasure and
pain, the undeluded reach the eternal abode.

6. Neither the Sun, the Moon, nor fire lights up My eternal abode. Those who reach there, never return.

7. The living entities in this world are an eternal part of Me. Being firmly attached to the material nature, they struggle with the senses and the mind.

8. Whatever body the Lord takes on, He always carries the senses and the mind when He leaves it, just as the breeze carries fragrance from its source.

9. *śrotraṁ cakṣuḥ sparśanaṁ ca*
rasanaṁ ghrāṇam eva ca
adhiṣṭhāya manaś cāyaṁ
viśayān upasevate

10. *utkrāmantaṁ sthitaṁ vāpi*
bhuñjānaṁ vā guṇānvitam
vimūḍhā nānupaśyanti
paśyanti jñāna-cakṣuṣaḥ

11. *yatanto yoginaś cainaṁ*
paśyanty ātmany avasthitam
yatanto' py akṛtātmāno
nainaṁ paśyanty acetasaḥ

12. *yad āditya-gataṁ tejo*
jagad bhāsayate' khilam
yac candramasi yac cāgnau
tat tejo viddhi mamakam

13. *gām āviśya ca bhūtāni*
dhārayāmy aham ojasā
puṣṇāmi cauṣadhīḥ sarvāḥ
somo bhūtvā rasātmakaḥ

14. *ahaṁ vaiśvānaro bhūtvā*
prāṇināṁ deham āśritaḥ
prāṇāpāna-samāyuktaḥ
pacāmy annaṁ catur-vidham

15. *sarvasya cāhaṁ hṛdi samniviṣṭo*
mattaḥ smṛtir jñānam apohanaṃ ca
vedaiś ca sarvair aham eva vedyo
vedānta-kṛd veda-vid eva cāham

16. *dvāv imau puruṣau loke*
kṣaraś cākṣara eva ca
kṣaraḥ sarvāṇi bhūtāni
kūṭa-stho' kṣara ucyate

9. The Lord takes his stand upon hearing, sight, taste, touch, smell and the mind. He enjoys sense-objects.

10. The deluded cannot understand how He leaves the body, nor while remaining in the body how He is enjoying the material qualities. But those who see through transcendental knowledge can, actually see.

11. Striving ascetics can perceive the Lord situated in the self. But the imprudent, who have unformed minds, although endeavouring, cannot see Him.

12. Understand that the brightness which is in the Sun, which illumines the Earth, which is in the Moon and in fire comes from Me.

13. I enter the Earth and I sustain all living beings by My energy. I become *soma*, the essence of essences, that nourishes all plants.

14. I am the fire of digestion in the bodies of all living beings; mixed with the air of life, inhaled and exhaled, I digest the four kinds of food.

15. And I am situated in everyone's heart. From Me come universal wisdom, memory and forgetfulness. I am that which is to be known by all the Vedas. I am also the knower of the Vedas and author of Vedanta.

16. There are two kinds of beings in the world, the perishable and the imperishable. All beings are perishable. They become known as imperishable when they are joined in the Supreme.

17. *uttamaḥ puruṣas tv anyaḥ*
paramātmety udāhṛtaḥ
yo loka-trayam āviśya
bibharty avyaya īśvaraḥ

18. *yasmāt kṣaram atīto' ham*
akṣarād api cottamaḥ
ato'smi loke vede ca
prathitaḥ puruṣottamah

19. *yo mām evam asammūḍho*
jānāti puruṣottamam
sa sarva-vid bhajati māṁ
sarva-bhāvena bhārata

20. *iti guhyatamaṁ śāstram*
idam uktaṁ mayānagha
etad buddhvā buddhimān syāt
kṛta-kṛtyaś ca bhārata

17. But, other than those two, is the Supreme Spirit, called the highest being, the imperishable Lord, who pervades and sustains the three worlds.

18. I surpass the perishable; I am higher than the imperishable. I am, therefore, known as the highest being in the world and in the Vedas.

19. Those who are undeluded knowing that I am the highest being, know everything. They worship Me with all their heart.

20. Sinless one, to you I have spoken about the most secret scriptures. One who knows this, becomes wise, and one's endeavours become perfect, Bharata.

Chapter Sixteen

Two Kinds of Human Nature

The Lord describes the qualities of one born with divine nature and also those with the demoniac nature. Following the path of sense gratification, under the spell of delusion, they fall into the demoniac races through the gates of hell, desire, anger and greed, into the lowest mode of existence. Therefore, one should let scripture be the guide for correct action.

Śrī Bhagavān uvāca

1. *abhayaṁ sattva saṁśuddhir*
jñāna-yoga-vyavasthitiḥ
dānaṁ samaś ca yajñaś ca
svādhyayās tapa ārjavam

2. *ahiṁsā satyam akrodhas*
tyāgah śāntir apaiśunam
dayā bhūtesv aloluptvaṁ
mārdavaṁ hrīr acāpalam

3. *tejaḥ kṣamā dhṛtiḥ śaucam*
adroho nāti-mānitā
bhavanti sampadaṁ daivīm
abhijātasya bhārata

4. *dambho darpo' bhimānaś ca*
krodhaḥ pāruṣyam eva ca
ajñānaṁ cābhijātasya
pārtha sampadam āsurīm

5. *daivī sampad vimokṣāya*
nibandhāyāsurī matā
mā śucāḥ saṁpadaṁ daivīm
abhijāto' si pāṇḍava

6. *dvau bhūta-sargau loke' smin*
daiva āsura eva ca
daivo vistaraśaḥ prokta
āsuraṁ pārtha me śṛṇu

7. *pravṛttiṁ ca nivṛttiṁ ca*
janā na vidur āsurāḥ
na śaucaṁ nāpi cācāro
na satyaṁ teṣu vidyate

8. *asatyam apratiṣṭhaṁ te*
jagad āhur anīśvaram
aparaspara-sambhūtaṁ
kim anyat kāma-haitukam

The Lord said:

1-3. Bravery, purity of nature, developing spiritual understanding, giving in charity, self-control, prayer and recitation of sacred texts, non-violence, truthfulness, freedom from anger and desire, renunciation, peacefulness, uprightness, compassion and leniency towards all beings, freedom from greed, gentleness, modesty, steadfastness, spiritual influence, forgiveness, constancy, purity of mind, freedom from treachery and pride, all these belong to one who is born to attain the divine, Bharata.

4. Hypocrisy, arrogance, conceit, anger, insult and ignorance, belong to one who is born for demoniac deeds, Partha.

5. Divine deeds lead to liberation, demoniac ones to bondage, but do not worry, Pandava, you are born for divine deeds.

6. There are two kinds of created beings in this world, Partha, the divine and the demoniac. I have told you in detail of the divine. Now hear from Me of the demoniac.

7. Demoniac people do not know what should be done and what should not be done. Neither purity of mind, nor good behaviour, nor truth exists in them.

8. They say this world is unreal, without God, and has no foundation. It is produced by lust, nothing more nor less.

9. *etāṁ dṛṣṭim avaṣṭabhya*
naṣṭātmāno' lpa-buddhayaḥ
prabhavanty ugra-karmāṇaḥ
kṣayāya jagato' hitāḥ

10. *kāmam āśritya duṣpūraṁ*
dambha-māna-madānvitāḥ
mohād gṛhītvāsad-grāhān
pravartante' śuci-vratāḥ

11. *cintām aparimeyāṁ ca*
pralayāntām upāśritāḥ
kāmopabhoga-paramā
etāvad iti niścitāḥ

12. *āśā-pāśa-śatair baddhāḥ*
kāma-krodha-parāyaṇāḥ
īhante kāma-bhogārtham
anyāyenārtha-sañcayān

13. *idam adya mayā labdham*
imaṁ prāpsye manoratham
idam astīdam api me
bhaviṣyati punar dhanam

14. *asau mayā hataḥ śatrur*
haniṣye cāparān api
īśvaro' ham ahaṁ bhogī
siddho' haṁ balavān sukhī

15. *āḍhyo' bhijanavān asmi*
ko' nyo' sti sadṛśo mayā
yakṣye dāsyāmi modiṣya
ity ajñana-vimohitāḥ

16. *aneka-citta-vibhrāntā*
moha-jāla-samāvṛtāḥ
prasaktāḥ kāma-bhogeṣu
patanti narake' sucau

9. Accepting this theory, these less intelligent people, flourish as enemies of the world engaged in harmful activities that destroy it.

10. Taking shelter of insatiable desire, endowed with hypocrisy, pride and arrogance, holding evil through delusion, they commit themselves to an impure life.

11. They cling to unlimited anxieties, ending only in death. Sensual gratifications are their highest aim and they are determined that is all there is.

12. Fettered by hundreds of hopes, and absorbed in desires and resentments, they endeavour to accumulate wealth by unjust means, for the purpose of sense gratification.

13. Beguiled by ignorance they think, "To-day I have taken this to fulfil my desire. This is mine, and that also. Tomorrow my wealth will grow more and more."

14. "I have slain that enemy, and I shall slay others also. I am a Lord, I enjoy, I am successful, I am powerful, I am prosperous."

15. "I am wealthy, and of noble descent. Who is my equal? I will sacrifice, offer gifts and I will rejoice."

16. Confused by many aims, caught in the net of delusion, attached to sense gratification, they fall into a foul hell.

17. *ātma-saṁbhāvitāḥ stabdhā*
dhana-māna-madānvitāḥ
yajante nāma-yajñais te
dambhenāvidhi-pūrvakam

18. *ahaṅkāraṁ balaṁ darpaṁ*
kāmaṁ krodhaṁ ca saṁśritāḥ
mām ātma-para-deheṣu
pradviṣanto' bhyasūyakāḥ

19. *tān ahaṁ dviṣataḥ krūrān*
saṁsāreṣu narādhamān
kṣipāmy ajasram aśubhān
āsurīṣv eva yoniṣu

20. *āsurīm yonim āpannā*
mūḍhā janmani janmani
mām aprāpyaiva kaunteya
tato yānty adhamāṁ gatim

21. *tri-vidhaṁ narakasyedaṁ*
dvāraṁ nāśanam ātmanaḥ
kāmaḥ krodhas tathā lobhas
tasmād etat trayaṁ tyajet

22. *etair vimuktaḥ kaunteya*
tamo-dvārais tribhir naraḥ
ācaraty ātmanaḥ śreyas
tato yāti parāṁ gatim

23. *yaḥ śāstra-vidhim utsṛjya*
vartate kāma-kārataḥ
na sa siddhim avāpnoti
na sukhaṁ na parāṁ gatim

24. *tasmāc chāstraṁ pramāṇaṁ te*
kāryākārya-vyavasthitau
jñātvā śāstra-vidhānoktaṁ
karma kartum ihārhasi

17. Conceited, arrogant, proud of their wealth, they perform sacrifice in name only out of hypocrisy, not according to the rules.

18. They adhere to egoism, pride of strength, lust and anger. These envious people hate Me in their own bodies and those of others.

19. These hostile, cruel, vilest of people in the world, I cast into the vicious, demoniac races for ever.

20. Birth after birth, these foolish beings enter into the demoniac races, without ever reaching Me. Eventually they descend to the lowest mode of existence, Kaunteya.

21. The three gates of hell, desire, anger and greed, destroy the self, therefore, one should avoid them.

22. Being free from these three gates of darkness, son of Kunti, a person can do what is good for his own self, and thus advance towards ultimate perfection.

23. The person that disregards the teachings of the scriptures and lives according to his desires, neither attains perfection, nor happiness, nor the final destination.

24. Therefore, let the scriptures be your authority to determine what should be done and what should not be done. Knowing such commandments a person should do his duty in this world.

Chapter Seventeen

Three Kinds of Faith

There are three kinds of faith, foodstuffs, sacrifices, austerities, charity and sacred syllables for the performance of religious activities.

Arjuna uvāca

1. *ye śāstra-vidhim utsṛjya*
yajante śraddhayānvitāḥ
teṣāṁ niṣṭha tu ka kṛṣṇa
sattvam aho rajas tamaḥ

Śrī Bhagavān uvāca

2. *tri-vidhā bhavati śraddhā*
dehināṁ sā svabhāva-jā
sāttvikī rājasī caiva
tāmasī ceti tāṁ śṛṇu

3. *sattvānurūpā sarvasya*
śraddhā bhavati bhārata
śraddhā-mayo' yaṁ puruṣo
yo yac-chraddhaḥ sa eva saḥ

4. *yajante sāttvikā devān*
yakṣa-rakṣāṁsi rājasāḥ
pretān bhūta-gaṇāṁś cānye
yajante tāmasā janāḥ

5. *aśāstra-vihitaṁ ghoraṁ*
tapyante ye tapo janāḥ
dambhāhaṅkāra-saṁyuktāḥ
kāma-rāga-balānvitāḥ

6. *karśayantaḥ śarīra-sthaṁ*
bhūta-grāmam acetasaḥ
māṁ caivāntaḥśarīra-sthaṁ
tān viddhy āsura-niścayān

7. *āhāras tv api sarvasya*
tri-vidho bhavati priyaḥ
yajñas tapas tathā dānaṁ
teṣāṁ bhedam imaṁ śṛṇu

Arjuna said:

1. O Krishna, what of those who disregard the commandments of the scriptures, but worship with steady faith? Are they in goodness, passion, or ignorance?

The Lord said:

2. There are three kinds of faith according to the nature of the person, goodness, passion, or ignorance. Now hear about this.

3. One's faith is according to one's nature, Bharata. A person's faith determines what he truly is.

4. People in the nature of goodness worship the demigods; those in the nature of passion worship the demons; and the others, in the nature of ignorance, worship the spirits of the dead and the multitude of ghosts.

5. Those who perform dreadful, unscriptural austerities are associated with hypocrisy and egoism. They are driven by desire and passion.

6. They senselessly torment the elements of the body, and even Me, Who dwells within the body. Be aware, they are certainly demoniac.

7. There are also three kinds of food preferences, as there are sacrifices, austerities, and charity. Hear now of these differences.

8. *āyuḥ-sattva-balārogya-*
sukha-prīti-vivardhanāḥ
rasyāḥ snigdhāḥ sthirā hṛdyā
āhārāḥ sāttvika-priyāḥ

9. *kaṭv-amla-lavaṇāty-uṣṇa*
tīkṣṇa-rūkṣa-vidāhinaḥ
āhārā rājasasyeṣṭā
duḥkha-śokāmaya-pradāḥ

10. *yāta-yāmaṁ gata-rasaṁ*
pūti paryuṣitaṁ ca yat
ucchiṣṭam api cāmedhyaṁ
bhojanaṁ tāmasa-priyam

11. *aphalākāṅkṣibhir yajño*
vidhi-dṛṣṭo ya ijyate
yaṣṭavyam eveti manaḥ
samādhāya sa sāttvikaḥ

12. *abhisamdhāya tu phalaṁ*
dambhārtham api caiva yat
ijyate bharata-śreṣṭha
taṁ yajñaṁ viddhi rājasam

13. *vidhi-hīnam asṛṣṭānnaṁ*
mantra-hīnam adakṣiṇam
śraddhā-virahitaṁ yajñaṁ
tāmasaṁ paricakṣate

14. *deva-dvija-guru-prājña-*
pūjanaṁ śaucam ārjavam
brahmacaryam ahiṁsā ca
śārīram tapa ucyate

15. *anudvega-karaṁ vākyaṁ*
satyaṁ priya-hitaṁ ca yat
svādhyāyābhyasanaṁ caiva
vāṅ-mayaṁ tapa ucyate

8. Those in the nature of goodness, like food that invigorates longevity, vitality, endurance, health, happiness and joy, that are tasty, fatty, substantial and pleasant to the stomach.

9. Those in the nature of passion, like foods that are bitter, sour, salty, very hot, pungent, dry and burning. Such foods cause uneasiness, pain and sickness.

10. Those in the nature of ignorance, like foods that are stale, tasteless, bad smelling, rotting, impure and rejected.

11. Those, who perform sacrifices as directed in scripture, without desiring reward, with their mind fixed intently are in the nature of goodness.

12. But that sacrifice which is performed out of pride, or for gain, know Bharata, is in the nature of passion.

13. It is said a sacrifice is in the nature of ignorance which is without scriptural reference, in which no *prasada* is distributed, no sacred hymns recited, no gifts offered to the priests, and which is lacking in faith.

14. To honour God, the *brahmanas*, the spiritual preceptors, learned men, and to be pure of mind, honest, chaste and non-violent, are called austerities of the body.

15. To speak words that do not cause anxiety, words that are true, agreeable and beneficial, and to study and recite any sacred text, this is known as austerity of speech.

16. *manaḥ-prasādaḥ saumyatvaṁ*
maunam ātma-vinigrahaḥ
bhāva-saṁśudhir ity etat
tapo mānasam ucyate

17. *śraddhayā parayā taptaṁ*
tapas tat tri-vidhaṁ naraiḥ
aphalākāṅkṣibhir yuktaiḥ
sāttvikaṁ paricakṣate

18. *satkāra-māna-pūjartham*
tapo dambhena caiva yat
kriyate tad iha proktaṁ
rājasaṁ calam adhruvam

19. *mūḍha-grāheṇātmano yat*
pīḍayā kriyate tapaḥ
parasyotsādanārthaṁ vā
tat tāmasam udāhṛtam

20. *dātavyam iti yad dānaṁ*
dīyate'nupakāriṇe
deśe kāle ca pātre ca
tad dānaṁ sāttvikaṁ smṛtam

21. *yat tu pratyupakārārthaṁ*
phalam uddiśya vā punaḥ
dīyate ca parikliṣṭaṁ
tad dānaṁ rājasaṁ smṛtam

22. *adeśa-kāle yad dānam*
apātrebhyaś ca dīyate
asat-kṛtam avajñātaṁ
tat tāmasam udāhṛtam

23. *oṁ tat sad iti nirdeśo*
brahmanas tri-vidhaḥ smṛtaḥ
brāhmaṇās tena vedāś ca
yajñāś ca vihitāḥ purā

16. Peace of mind
Benevolence
Silence
Self-control
Purification of one's existence—
This is known as mental austerity.

17. This three-fold austerity, practised with utmost faith by people who are spiritually disciplined, without desiring reward, is called austerity in the nature of goodness.

18. Austerity practised with hypocrisy, for the sake of gaining favour, honour or reverence, is austerity in the nature of passion. It is neither steady nor reliable.

19. The practice of austerity that is misguided, involving self-torment, or for the purpose of injuring someone, is declared to be in the nature of ignorance.

20. Charity that is made to a worthy person, in the right place and time, without expectation of a return, is considered to be in the nature of goodness.

21. Charity that is made with expectation of a return, or for the sake of gain, or made with reluctance, is considered to be in the nature of passion.

22. Charity that is made to an unfit recipient, or at the wrong place and time, or with offence, or contempt, is said to be in the nature of ignorance.

23. God is indicated by the three words, Om Tat Sat—God, the ultimate reality, underlying all phenomena to whom the *brahmanas*, the Vedas and sacrifices were hitherto consecrated.

24. *tasmād oṁ ity udāhṛtya*
yajña-dāna-tapaḥ-kriyāḥ
pravartante vidhānoktāḥ
satataṁ brahma-vādinām

25. *tad ity anabhisamdhāya*
phalaṁ yajña-tapaḥ-kriyāḥ
dāna-kriyāś ca vividhāḥ
kriyante mokṣa-kāṅkṣibhiḥ

26. *sad-bhāve sādhu-bhāve ca*
sad ity etat prayujyate
praśaste karmaṇi tathā
sac-chabdaḥ pārtha yujyate

27. *yajñe tapasi dāne ca*
sthitiḥ sad iti cocyate
karma caiva tad-arthīyaṁ
sad ity evābhidhīyate

28. *aśraddhayā hutaṁ dattaṁ*
tapas taptaṁ kṛtaṁ ca yat
asad ity ucyate pārtha
na ca tat pretya no iha

24. Therefore, the followers of the Vedas always begin acts of sacrifice, charity and austerity, by uttering the mystic monosyllable Om.

25. Those who perform acts of sacrifice, austerity and various acts of charity with the word Tat—that—desiring no reward, will attain liberation.

26. The word Sat—good and real—leads to truth and goodness, Partha. Sat is also connected with all auspicious acts.

27. Constancy in sacrifice, austerity, and charity is also called Sat. Action for the sake of Tat—God—is also called Sat.

28. Whatever is given, or performed in sacrifice, or practised in penance without faith, is called Asat—unreal. It is worth-nothing, either in this world or the next, Partha.

Chapter Eighteen

Renunciation and Detachment

Krishna concludes by describing the three kinds of actions, the five causes of action, the three kinds of knowledge, qualities, intelligence, determination, happiness and duties. By following the activities of one's nature one can achieve success, perfection, and through devotion one can attain the eternal, blissful abode of the Lord. So ends this greatest conversation of all time between the Supreme Lord and man.

Arjuna uvāca

1. *sannyāsasya mahā-bāho*
tattvam icchāmi veditum
tyāgasya ca hṛṣīkesa
pṛthak keś-iniṣūdanna

Śrī Bhagavān uvāca

2. *kāmyānāṁ karmaṇāṁ nyāsaṁ*
samnyāsaṁ kavayo viduḥ
sarva-karma-phala-tyāgaṁ
prāhus tyāgaṁ vicakṣaṇāḥ

3. *tyājyaṁ doṣ-avad ity eke*
karma prāhur manīṣiṇaḥ
yajña-dāna-tapaḥ-karma
na tyājyam iti cāpare

4. *niścayaṁ śṛṇu me tatra*
tyāge bharata-sattama
tyāgo hi puruṣa-vyāghra
tri-vidhaḥ samprakīrtitaḥ

5. *yajña-dāna-tapaḥ-karma*
na tyājyaṁ kāryam eva tat
yajño dānaṁ tapaś caiva
pāvanāni manīṣiṇām

6. *etāny api tu karmāṇi*
saṅgaṁ tyaktvā phalāni ca
kartavyānīti me pārtha
niścitaṁ matam uttamam

7. *niyatasya tu samnyāsaḥ*
karmaṇo nopapadyate
mohāt tasya parityāgas
tāmasaḥ parikīritaḥ

Arjuna said:

1. O mighty-armed, I wish to know the truth of renunciation and also of detachment, O Lord of the senses, slayer of the demon Kesi.

The Lord said:

2. Giving up selfishly motivated activities, the sages understand as renunciation. Giving up the fruits of all activities, the wise declare as detachment.

3. Some wise men say that all activities should be given up as transgression; but others say acts of sacrifice, charity, and religious austerity should not be given up.

4. Now hear with certainty My opinion on the subject of detachment, best of Bharatas. Detachment is declared to be three-fold, O best of men.

5. Acts of sacrifice, charity and austerity should not be given up, but should be performed. Sacrifice, charity and austerity purify even the wise.

6. These activities should be performed, Arjuna, but without attachment or desire for benefit. They should be performed as duty. This is definitely My highest opinion.

7. It is never justified to give up prescribed activites. Giving them up out of delusion, is said to be in the nature of ignorance.

8. *duḥkham ity eva yat karma*
kaya-kleśa-bhayāt tyajet
sa kṛtvā rājasaṁ tyāgaṁ
naiva tyāga-phalaṁ labhet

9. *kāṛyam ity eva yat karma*
niyataṁ kriyate' rjuna
sangaṁ tyaktvā phalaṁ caiva
sa tyāgaḥ sāttviko mataḥ

10. *na dveṣṭy akuśalaṁ karma*
kuśale nānuṣajjate
tyāgī sattva-samāviṣṭo
medhāvī chinna-saṁśayaḥ

11. *na hi deha-bhṛtā śakyaṁ*
tyaktuṁ karmāṇy aśeṣataḥ
yas tu karma-phala-tyāgī
sa tyāgīty abhidhīyate

12. *aniṣṭam īṣṭaṁ miśraṁ ca*
tri-vidhaṁ karmaṇaḥ phalam
bhavaty atyāgināṁ pretya
na tu sannyāsināṁ kvacit

13. *pañcaitāni mahā-bāho*
kāraṇāni nibodha me
sāṅkhye kṛtānte proktāni
siddhaye sarva-karmaṇm

14. *adhiṣṭhānaṁ tathā kartā*
karaṇaṁ ca pṛtha-gvidham
vividhāś ca pṛthak ceṣṭā
daivam caivātra pañcamam

15. *śarīra-vāṅ-manobhir yat*
karma prārabhate naraḥ
nyāyyaṁ vā viparitaṁ vā
pañcaite tasya hetavaḥ

8. The person who gives up prescribed activities because of difficulty or fear of bodily suffering, renounces in the nature of passion. Nothing is obtained from such renunciation.

9. When prescribed activities are performed as duty with detachment from any benefit, that renunciation is in the nature of goodness, Arjuna.

10. A confident and intelligent renouncer, endowed with the nature of goodness, is neither attached to auspicious activities nor dislikes inauspicious activities.

11. It is truly impossible for a living person to renounce activites completely, but he who renounces the fruits of activites is a true renouncer.

12. In the life to come, the three-fold results of action—undesired, desired, or mixed—await those unable to renounce. But for those who are renounced, there are no such results.

13. Now just learn from Me, mighty warrior. In the *sankhya* philosophy, based on the dualism of matter and soul, it is stated that there are five causes in the fulfilment of all activities.

14. The body, the doer, the various means by which an activity is performed, the different sorts of activites, and the fifth is the Supreme, God.

15. Whatever activity, right or wrong, one undertakes with body, speech or mind, these five are its causes.

16. *tatraivaṁ sati kartāram*
ātmānaṁ kevalaṁ tu yaḥ
paśyaty akṛta-buddhitvān
na sa paśyati durmatiḥ

17. *yasya nāhaṅkṛto bhāvo*
buddhir yasya na lipyate
hatvāpi sa imāl lokān
na hanti na nibadhyate

18. *jñānaṁ jñeyaṁ parijñātā*
tri-vidhā-karma-codanā
karaṇaṁ karma karteti
tri-vidhaḥ karma-saṅgrahaḥ

19. *jñānaṁ karma ca kartā ca*
tridhaiva guṇa-bhedataḥ
procyate guṇa-sankhayāne
yathāvac chṛṇu tāny api

20. *sarva-bhūteṣu yenaikaṁ*
bhāvam avyayam īkṣate
avibhaktaṁ vibhakteṣu
taj jñānaṁ viddhi sattvikam

21. *pṛthaktvena tu yaj jñānaṁ*
nānā-bhāvān pṛthag-vidhān
vetti sarveṣu bhūteṣu
taj jñānaṁ viddhi rājasam

22. *yat tu kṛtsna-vad ekasmin*
kārye saktam ahaitukam
atattvārtha-vad alpaṁ ca
tat tāmasam udāhṛtam

23. *niyataṁ saṅga-rahitam*
arāga-dveṣataḥ kṛtam
aphala-prepsunā karma
yat tat sāttvikam ucyate

16. Foolish people, due to ignorance, cannot see this. They see themselves as the only doer.

17. A person of unegoistic nature and untainted intelligence, though he kills these men here, he does not kill them and is not bound by these activities.

18. Knowledge, the knowable object and the knower are the three motives that impel action. The senses, activity and the doer are the three constituents of action.

19. The theory of the three principles of nature declares that there are three kinds of knowledge, activities and doers, each according to their different qualities. Hear about them also.

20. That knowledge, by which one sees the imperishable Being in all beings, the undivided in the divided, know that knowledge to be in the nature of goodness.

21. But that knowledge, by which one sees different kinds of entities in all the different living beings, know that knowledge to be in the nature of passion.

22. And that knowledge which takes one activity to be all in all, which has no cause, which is trivial and does not conform with the nature of truth, is said to be in the nature of ignorance.

23. Prescribed activity, performed without attachment, love or hatred by someone desiring no recompense, is known to be in the nature of goodness.

24. *yat tu kāmepsunā karma*
sāhaṅkāreṇa vā punaḥ
kriyate bahulāyāsaṁ
tad rājasam udāhṛtam

25. *anubandhaṁ kṣayaṁ hiṁsām*
anapekṣya ca pauruṣam
mohād ārabhyate karma
yat tat tāmasam ucyate

26. *mukta-saṅgo' nahaṁ-vādī*
dhṛty-utsāha-samanvitaḥ
siddhy-asiddhyor nirvikāraḥ
kartā sāttvika ucyate

27. *rāgī karma-phala-prepsur*
lubdho hiṁsātmako' śuciḥ
harṣa-śokānvitaḥ kartā
rājasaḥ parikīrtitaḥ

28. *ayuktaḥ prākṛtaḥ stabdhaḥ*
śaṭho naiṣkṛtiko' lasaḥ
viṣādī dīrgha-sūtrī ca
kartā tāmasa ucyate

29. *buddher bhedaṁ dhṛteś caiva*
guṇatas tri-vidhaṁ śṛṇu
procyamānam aśeṣeṇa
pṛthaktvena dhanañjaya

30. *pravṛttiṁ ca nivṛttiṁ ca*
kāryākārye bhayābhaye
bandhaṁ mokṣaṁ ca yā vetti
buddhiḥ sā pārtha sāttvikī

31. *yayā dharmam adharmaṁ ca*
kāryaṁ cākāryam eva ca
ayathāvat prajāñati
buddhiḥ sā pārtha rājasī

24. Prescribed activity, performed with strenuous effort, or with egoism by someone desirous of sensual results, is said to be in the nature of passion.

25. Prescribed activity, undertaken through delusion, irrespective of consequence, loss, injury and one's own ability, is said to be in the nature of ignorance.

26. Free from worldly attachment, conceit or pride, fully endowed with strength of will, resolution, remaining unchanged in success or failure, such a person is declared to be in the nature of goodness.

27. Impure, cruel, greedy, impassioned for the fruits of activities, moved by joy and sorrow, such person is said to be in the nature of passion.

28. Without devotion, unrefined, stubborn, malignant, dishonest, lazy, despondent and tardy, such a one is said to be in the nature of ignorance.

29. Listen, winner of wealth, as I now declare fully and distinctly the varieties of intelligence and resolve, according to the three-fold qualities of all beings.

30. That intelligence which knows activity and inactivity, what is to be done and not to be done, danger and security, mundane bondage and eternal emancipation, is in the nature of goodness, Arjuna.

31. Intelligence that misconceives right and wrong, what is to be done and what is not to be done, that intelligence, Partha, is in the nature of passion.

32. *adharmaṁ dharmam iti yā*
manyate tamasāvṛtā
sarvārthān viparītāṁś ca
buddhiḥ sa pārtha tāmasī

33. *dhṛtyā yayā dhārayate*
manaḥ-prāṇendriya-kriyāḥ
yogenāvyabhicāriṇyā
dhṛtiḥ sā pārtha sāttvikī

34. *yayā tu dharma-kāmarthān*
dhṛtyā dhārayate' rjuna
prasaṅgena phalākāṅkṣī
dhṛtiḥ sā pārtha rājasī

35. *yayā svapnaṁ bhayaṁ śokaṁ*
viṣādaṁ madam eva ca
na vimuñcati durmedhā
dhṛtiḥ sā pārtha tāmasī

36. *sukhaṁ tv idānīṁ tri-vidhaṁ*
śṛṅu me bharatarṣabha
abhyāsād ramate yatra
duḥkhāntaṁ ca nigacchati

37. *yat tad agre viṣam iva*
pariṇāme' mṛtopamam
tat sukhaṁ sāttvikaṁ proktam
ātma-buddhi-prasāda-jam

38. *viṣayendriya-saṁyogād*
yat tad agre' mṛtopamam
pariṇāme viṣam iva
tat sukhaṁ rājasaṁ smṛtam

39. *yad agre cānubandhe ca*
sukhaṁ mohanam ātmanaḥ
nidrālasya-pramādotthaṁ
tat tamasam udāhṛtam

32. That intelligence, veiled by mental darkness, which believes wrong to be right, and sees all things in a perverted way, is in the nature of ignorance.

33. Determination which controls the activities of the mind, breath and senses with unfailing spiritual discipline, that determination is in the nature of goodness, Partha.

34. But determination by which one clings to righteousness, desire and wealth because of attachment, being eager for reward, that determination is in the nature of passion, Partha.

35. Determination by which the dull-witted person, does not give up dreaming, fear, sorrow, despair and pride, that determination is in the nature of ignorance, Partha.

36. Now hear from Me, O prince, about the three kinds of happiness, by which through steady practice, one may delight and even reach the end of all sorrows.

37. Happiness, born from the purity of self-knowledge, that seems like poison in the beginning and like nectar in the end, that happiness is said to be in the nature of goodness.

38. Happiness that comes from contact of the senses with the sense objects, that seems like nectar in the beginning but poison in the end, that happiness is said to be in the nature of passion.

39. Happiness that comes from sleep, laziness or negligence, deluding the self from beginning to end, that happiness is said to be in the nature of ignorance.

40. *na tad asti pṛthivyaṁ vā*
divi deveṣu vā punaḥ
sattvaṁ prakṛti-jair muktaṁ
yad ebhiḥ syāt tribhir guṇaiḥ

41. *brāhmaṇa-kṣatriya-viśāṁ*
śūdrāṇāṁ ca paramtapa
karmani pravibhaktani
svabhāva-prabhavair guṇaiḥ

42. *śamo damas tapaḥ śaucaṁ*
kṣāntir ārjavam eva ca
jñānaṁ vijñānam āstikyaṁ
brahma-karma svabhāva-jam

43. *śauryaṁ tejo dhrtir dākṣyaṁ*
yuddhe cāpy apalāyanam
dānam īśvara-bhāvaś ca
kṣātraṁ-karma svabhāva-jam

44. *kṛṣi-go-rakṣya-vāṇijyaṁ*
vaiśya-karma svabhāva-jam
paricaryātmakam karma
śūdrasyāpi svabhāva-jam

45. *sve sve karmaṇy abhirataḥ*
saṁsiddhiṁ labhate naraḥ
sva-karma-nirataḥ siddhiṁ
yathā vindati tac chṛṇu

46. *yataḥ pravṛttir bhūtānāṁ*
yena sarvam idaṁ tatam
sva-karmaṇā tam abhyarcya
siddhiṁ vindati mānavaḥ

47. *śreyān-sva-dharmo viguṇaḥ*
para-dharmāt sv-anuṣthitāt
svabhāva-niyataṁ karma
kurvan nāpnoti kilbiṣam

40. There is no living being on earth or among the demigods in heaven, that can be free from these three qualities born of material nature.

41. The duties of the *brahmanas, ksatriyas, vaisyas* and *sudras,* O conqueror, are divided according to the qualities born of their own natures.

42. The activities of the *brahmanas* by nature show inner calm, self-control, austerity, purity of mind, forgiveness, honesty, sacred wisdom, knowledge and belief in God.

43. Valour, strength, firmness, skill, fearlessness in battle, generosity and leadership, are the activities born of the *ksatriyas* nature.

44. Cow protection, agriculture and trade are by nature the activities of the *vaisyas,* and service to others is the activity which forms the nature of the *sudras.*

45. One who follows the activities of his own nature meets with success. Listen, how devotion to one's own activities leads to perfection.

46. One who worships with one's own activities, He from Whom all living beings originate and by Whom everything is pervaded, meets with success.

47. It is better to be imperfect in one's own duty than perfect in someone else's duty. One commits no offence when performing one's own duty established by one's nature.

48. *saha-jaṁ karma kaunteya*
sa-doṣam api na tyajet
sarvārambhā hi doṣeṇa
dhūmenāgnir ivāvṛtāḥ

49. *asakta-buddhiḥ sarvatra*
jitātmā vigata-spṛhaḥ
naiṣkarmya-siddhiṁ paramāṁ
saṁnyāsenādhigacchati

50. *siddhiṁ prāpto yathā brahma*
tathāpnoti nibodha me
samāsenaiva kaunteya
niṣṭhā jñānasya yā parā

51. *buddhyā viśuddhayā yukto*
dhṛtyātmānaṁ niyamya ca
śabdādīn viṣayāṁs tyaktvā
rāga-dveṣau vyudasya ca

52. *vivikta-sevī laghv-āśī*
yata-vāk-kāya-mānasaḥ
dhyāna-yoga-paro nityaṁ
vairāgyaṁ samupāśritaḥ

53. *ahaṅkāraṁ balaṁ darpaṁ*
kāmaṁ krodhaṁ parigraham
vimucya nirmamaḥ śānto
brahma-bhūyāya kalpate

54. *brahma-bhūtaḥ prasannātmā*
na śocati na kāṅkṣati
samaḥ sarveṣu bhūteṣu
mad-bhaktiṁ labhate parām

55. *bhaktyā mām abhijānāti*
yāvān yaś cāsmi tattvataḥ
tato māṁ tattvato jñātvā
viśate tad-anantaram

48. Despite mistakes, O Kaunteya, one should not abondon the duty for which one is born. Mistakes surround all undertakings, as smoke surrounds fire.

49. Detached from passions, always subdued, devoid of desires, renouncing worldly concerns, one attains the highest freedom from actions and their conquences.

50. Having attained that perfection, learn from Me, concisely, son of Kunti, how one reaches *brahman,* the state of highest sacred knowledge.

51-53. Filled with pure intentions, firmly self-restrained, renouncing pleasure from sounds and sense-objects, casting off love and hatred, living in a lonely place, eating moderately, controlling speech, body and mind, constantly engrossed in profound meditation, resorting to freedom from worldly desires. Free from egoism, false strength, sensuality, anger and possessions, unselfish and undisturbed, such a person is fit to reach *brahman.*

54. Having reached *brahman,* this tranquil soul neither grieves nor desires, being equal to all living beings, he enters into My supreme devotion.

55. Through devotion, one recognises Me, My greatness and Who I am in truth. Thus, by knowing Me truly, one enters instantly into My abode.

56. *sarva-karmāṇy api sadā*
kurvāṇo mad-vyapāśrayaḥ
mat-prasādād avāpnoti
śāśvataṁ padam avyayam

57. *cetasā sarva-karmāṇi*
mayi saṁnyasya mat-paraḥ
buddhi-yogam upāśritya
mac-cittaḥ satataṁ bhava

58. *mac-cittaḥ sarva-durgāṇi*
mat-prasādāt tariṣyasi
atha cet tvam ahaṁkārān
na śroṣyasi vinaṅkṣyasi

59. *yad ahaṅkāram āśritya*
na yotsya iti manyase
mithyaiṣa vyavasāyas te
prakṛtis tvāṁ niyokṣyati

60. *svabhāva-jena kaunteya*
nibaddhaḥ svena karmaṇā
kartuṁ necchasi yan mohāt
kariṣyasy avaśo' pi tat

61. *īśvaraḥ sarva-bhūtānāṁ*
hṛd-deśe' rjuna tiṣṭhati
bhrāmayan sarva-bhutāni
yantrārūḍhāni māyayā

62. *tam eva śaraṇaṁ gaccha*
sarva-bhāvena bhārata
tat-prasādāt parāṁ śāntiṁ
sthānaṁ prāpsyasi śāśvatam

63. *iti te jñānam ākhyātaṁ*
guhyād guhyataraṁ mayā
vimṛśyaitad aśeṣeṇa
yathecchasi tathā kuru

56. Although one performs all kinds of work, one remains always dependent on Me, and by My grace attains the impersihable, eternal abode.

57. Surrender all your activities wholeheartedly to Me and be devoted to Me. Take shelter in intellectual awareness, with your mind always fully absorbed in Me.

58. Having your mind fixed on Me, by My grace, you will overcome all obstacles. But if, through arrogance, you do not listen, you will perish.

59. If you resort to pride and do not fight, thinking this decision is in vain, then you will be compelled to fight by your nature.

60. Although you do not wish to fight due to delusion, actions are born of your own nature, and you are bound to fight, even though unwillingly, Arjuna.

61. God is in the hearts of all living beings, Arjuna, prompting their movements by His supernatural power, as if they were fixed in a revolving machine of material nature.

62. Seek refuge in Him wholeheartedly, Bharata. By His grace, you will find supreme peace and the eternal abode.

63. This most secret, mysterious wisdom has, thus, been declared to you by Me. Now reflect on it fully, and then act as you wish.

64. *sarva-guhyatamaṁ bhūyaḥ*
śṛṇu me paramaṁ vacaḥ
iṣṭo' si me dṛḍham iti
tato vakṣyāmi te hitam

65. *man-manā bhava mad-bhakto*
mad-yājī māṁ namaskuru
mām evaiṣyasi satyaṁ te
pratijāne priyo' si me

66. *sarva-dharmān parityajya*
mām ekaṁ śaraṇaṁ vraja
ahaṁ tvā sarva-pāpebhyo
mokṣayiṣyāmi mā śucah

67. *idaṁ te nātapaskāya*
nābhaktāya kadācana
na cāśuśrūṣave vācyaṁ
na ca māṁ yo'bhyasūyati

68. *ya idaṁ paramaṁ guhyaṁ*
mad-bhakteṣv abhidhāsyati
bhaktiṁ mayi parāṁ kṛtvā
mām evaiṣyaty asaṁśayaḥ

69. *na ca tasmān manuṣyeṣu*
kaścin me priya-kṛttamaḥ
bhavitā na ca me tasmād
anyaḥ priyataro bhuvi

70. *adhyeṣyate ca ya imaṁ*
dharmyaṁ saṁvādam āvayoḥ
jñāna-yajñena tenāham
iṣṭaḥ syām iti me matiḥ

71. *śraddhāvan anasūyaś ca*
śṛṇuyād api yo naraḥ
so'pi muktaḥ śubhāl lokān
prāpnuyāt puṇya-karmaṇām

64. Listen once more to My supreme advice, the most confidential of all. Because you are very close to Me, and dearly beloved, I will, therefore, tell what is best for you.

65. Meditate on Me,
Be devoted to Me,
Worship Me,
Pay homage to Me,
I promise
You will certainly come to Me
Because you are most dear to Me.

66. Renounce all other obligations and take refuge in Me alone. I will liberate you from all sins. Do not worry.

67. This wisdom should never be spoken of by you to anyone who is irreligious, without devotion, unwilling to learn or hear, or who is envious of Me.

68. One who, in supreme love for Me, explains this most excellent mystery to My devotees, shall certainly come to Me.

69. No one renders Me more precious service than this. And no one will ever be dearer to Me in this world than he.

70. I also say that whoever studies this sacred conversation of ours, worships Me with wisdom.

71. And one who even listens to this with steady faith, free from envy, is also liberated, and will also reach the blissful worlds of the virtuous.

72. *kaccid etac chrutam pārtha*
tvayaikāgreṇa cetasā
kaccid ajñāna-sammohaḥ
pranaṣṭas te dhanañjaya

Arjuna uvāca

73. *naṣṭo mohaḥ smṛtir labdhā*
tvat-prasādān mayācyuta
sthito' smi gata-sandehaḥ
kariṣye vacanaṁ tava

Sañjaya uvāca

74. *ity ahaṁ vāsudevasya*
pārthasya ca mahātmanaḥ
saṁvādam imam aśrauṣam
adbhutaṁ roma-harṣaṇam

75. *vyāsa-prasādāc chrutavān*
etad guhyam ahaṁ param
yogaṁ yogeśvarāt kṛṣṇāt
sāksat kathayataḥ svayam

76. *rājan saṁsmṛtya saṁsmṛtya*
saṁvādam imam adbhutam
keśavārjunayoḥ puṇyaṁ
hṛṣyāmi ca muhur muhuḥ

77. *tac ca saṁsmṛtya saṁsmṛtya*
rūpam aty-adbhutaṁ hareḥ
vismayo me mahān rājan
hṛṣyāmi ca punaḥ punaḥ

78. *yatra yogeśvaraḥ kṛṣṇo*
yatra pārtho dhanur-dharaḥ
tatra srīr vijayo bhūtir
dhruvā nītir matir mama

72. Have you heard this with undivided attention, Partha? Has the delusion of your ignorance gone, Arjuna?

Arjuna said:

73. My delusion is gone. Through Your grace, my memory is restored, O imperishable Krishna. My doubts are dispelled; I am determined; I will do as You command.

Sanjaya said:

74. So I heard this wonderful conversation between Lord Krishna, son of Vasudeva, and the noble natured Partha, causing my hair to stand on end.

75. Through the kindness of the mystic sage Vyasa, I have heard Krishna, Lord of yoga, Himself explaining directly this supreme mystery.

76. O king, as often as I call to mind this marvellous and holy conversation between Lord Krishna and Arjuna, I am thrilled with joy again and again.

77. And as often as I bring back to mind that very wonderful form of Lord Krishna, O king, my astonishment is so great and I rejoice again and again.

78. Wherever there is Krishna, the Lord of yoga, and wherever there is the great archer, Arjuna, son of Partha, there will surely be grace, glory, prosperity and powerful morality. This is my belief.

Bibliography

Bhaktivedanta, A.C. Swami Prabhupada, *Bhagavad-Gita As It Is*, Hong Kong, Bhaktivedanta Book Trust, 1989

Brown, Lesley, *The New Shorter Oxford English Dictionary On Historical Principles, The New Authority On The English Language*, Vol 1-2, New York, Oxford University Press, 1993

Macdonell, Arthur A., *A Sanskrit Grammer for Students*, Delhi, Motilal Banarsidass Publishers Pvt. Ltd,, 2003

Mascaro, Juan, *The Bhagavad Gita, Translated from the Sanskrit with an Introduction By Simon Brodbeck*, London, Penguin Group, 2003

Monier-Williams, Sir Monier M.A., K.C.I.E., *A Sanskrit-English Dictionary*, New York, Oxford University Press, 1998

Sathya Sai Baba, *Message of The Lord, As a Practical Philosophy, Based on The Bhagavad-Gita and The Teachings of Sathya Sai Baba*, third edn., Anantapur District, Andhra Pradesh, Sri Sathya Sai Books & Publications Trust, 2003

Sinclair, Gregg M., *A Source Book In Indian Philosophy*, edited by Sarvepalli Radhakrishnan and Charles A. Moore, Princeton, New Jersey, Princeton University Press, 1989

Swami Chidbhavananda, *The Bhagavad-Gita And Commentary*, Tamil Nadu, Sri Ramakrishna Tapovanam (Publication Section), 1982

Swami Swarupananda, *Srimad Bhagavad-Gita*, Calcutta, Advaita Ashrama (Publication Department), 2000

Youngs, Homer S., *Translation by Baba*, Tustin, California, Sathya Sai Book, Center of America, 1975

Zaehner, R.C., *The Bhagavad-Gita With A Commentary Based On the Original Sources*, New York, Oxford University Press, 1973

Names of Lord Krishna in Bhagavad Gītā

ACHYUTA	The Indestructible.
ARISUDANA	Destroyer of foes.
BHAGAVAN	The Supreme Lord, who possesses the six divine qualities: omnipotence, righteousness, glory, grace, wisdom, detachment.
GOVINDA	One who has control over the animal nature in man. Lord who protects the cows.
HRISHIKESA	Lord of the senses.
ISVARA	God, the controller.
JAGAN-NIVASA	Abode or shelter of the world.
JANARDANA	One who uplifts humanity.
KESAVA	The Lord of Trinity, and He who has long black hair.
KESINISUDANA	Slayer of Kesi demon.
KRISHNA	Name of the eighth incarnation of Lord Vishnu. The maintainer of the universe.
MAHA-PURUSAH	The Supreme Spirit.
MADHAVA	Lord of the universe.
MADHUSUDANA	Destroyer of the demon Madhu.
PURUSHOTTAMA	The Highest Being.

VARSHNEYA	Descendant of the mighty Vrishnis' clan.
VASUDEVA	Soul of the universe.
LORD VISHNU	Who is all pervading, incarnating from age to age to protect and preserve all creation.
YADAVA	Descendant of the ancient hero called King Yadu.
YOGESWARA	Lord of yoga.

Names of Arjuna in Bhagavad Gītā

ANAGHA	Sinless person.
ARJUNA	Unblemished one, disciple of Lord Krishna.
BHARATARISHABHA	Prince of the Bharatas.
BHARATASATTAMA	The best of the Bharatas.
BHARATASRESHTHA	The best of the Bharatas.
DHANANJAYA	Conqueror of wealth.
GUDAKESA	Conqueror of sleep, ignorance.
KAPIDHVAJA	One who has the sign of Lord Hanumana on his banner.
KAUNTEYA	Son of Kunti.
KIRITI	One who wears the diadem.
KURUNANDANA	A descendant of the Kurus.
KURUSRESHTA	Best of the Kurus.
MAHABAHU	The mighty armed.
PANDAVA	Son of Pandu.
PARTHA	Son of Pritha, Kunti.
PARAMTAPA	Destroyer of foes.
PURUSHAVYGHIRA	A tiger among men.
SAVYASACHIN	One who is ambidexterous.